Artistry in Strings

Book 1

Parent's Guide

Wendy Barden

ISBN 0-8497-3410-X

© 2002 Kjos Music Press
4380 Jutland Drive, San Diego, California, 92117.
International copyright secured. All rights reserved. Printed in U. S. A.
WARNING! The contents of this publication are protected by copyright law.
To copy or reproduce any portion by any method is an infringement
of the copyright law. Anyone who reproduces copyrighted matter is subject
to substantial penalties and assessments for each infringement.

KJOS NEIL A. KJOS MUSIC COMPANY • San Diego, California

Table of Contents

About the Authors .... Inside Front Cover

Introduction 1
   Play a String Instrument? 1
   Your Child Needs Your Support 2
   About the Parent's Guide 3

Unit I — Ready, Set, Go! 4

Unit II — The D-String 13

Unit III — The A- and G-Strings 22

Unit IV — The C- and E-Strings 34

Unit V — Onward and Upward! 45

Reference 54
   Tuning the Instrument 54
   Practice Tips 57
   Instrument Care 58
   There's Always More To Learn! 59
   "Calling All Parents" from *The Instrumentalist* 60
   Blank manuscript paper (authorized for duplication) 62

48 Ways to Acknowledge an Exceptional Performance ... Inside Back Cover

Artistry in Strings
PARENT'S GUIDE

This Parent's Guide was written to help you — the parent, guardian, or other significant adult — support a special child's dream of playing a string instrument. Your child may be ready to explore new musical talents. She might be looking forward to meeting new friends, or feel ready for a new challenge. She may want to follow in the footsteps of an older sibling. Certainly everyone wants to be part of a satisfying and fun experience!

Playing a String Instrument?

Regardless of the initial attraction to a string instrument, there are many reasons to support your child's dream.

- According to neurologist Frank R. Wilson, "The child who is playing a musical instrument or singing on a regular basis is exercising the entire brain and stimulating general intelligence more than his or her counterpart who does not play or sing."

- Making music requires the development of higher-level thinking skills. Students are called on to analyze, create, evaluate, and make informed judgments.

- Self-discipline, confidence, and a sense of pride and personal worth grow out of meaningful musical experiences. When students perform on a string instrument, the joy of learning becomes real, tangible, and powerful.

- Participating in orchestra prepares people for the world of work by fostering skills identified as critical by the business community — independence, cooperation, team work, craftsmanship, responsibility, and leadership. The independent student-worker becomes capable of making decisions in situations where there are no standard answers.

- Music has value in and of itself, and plays a role in the human experience. Participation in orchestra will challenge and heighten aesthetic perception, and nourish the quest for beauty and self-expression.

2
Your Child Needs Your Support

To reach her full potential, your child needs you and your investment of time, money, and personal interest.

Time. Your child will progress more rapidly and confidently if the two of you are working side by side. With this Parent's Guide you will be able to assist often with home practicing. Put aside other work for a minute when your child has a new piece to share. Be available to provide transportation to lessons and rehearsals. Write the dates of her school concerts on the family calendar and be there to share in her accomplishments.

Money. The biggest expense you will incur when your child enrolls in the orchestra program is to rent or purchase an instrument. While there may be an instrument in the family that is available for her to play, your child must have an instrument that is the appropriate size. Keep in mind, too, as your child grows, you may need to get a larger instrument. Other items your child may need include:

- Music Stand
- Rosin
- Soft Cloth
- Pitch Pipe
- Shoulder Pad or Rock Stop
- *Artistry in Strings*, Book 1
- Manuscript Paper (may be duplicated from page 62 in this guide)
- Metronome
- *Artistry in Strings* CD Accompaniment Recordings
- *Artistry in Strings* Piano Accompaniment Book.

Your child's teacher can provide specific information on securing the items he or she wishes the students to have and use.

Personal Interest. Your genuine interest in your child's study of music, or lack of interest, will be very apparent. Get behind her but take it easy! There can be a fine line between supporting and pressuring; between enjoying your child's accomplishments and living through them. Your child will need your support when playing is fun, and all the encouragement you can muster when progress is a bit slower. One thing is certain—you will both enjoy sharing a love of music together!

About the Parent's Guide

Your child will receive regular instruction from her orchestra teacher using *Artistry in Strings* Book 1, by Robert Frost and Gerald Fischbach with Wendy Barden, but learning to play an instrument also requires practice outside of class. That's where you come in! Even if your own musical experience is limited, information in this guide will assist you in helping your child develop both skills and confidence playing her string instrument.

Activities and strategies throughout this guide will also help you support your child's growing understanding of music. They are aligned with the voluntary National Standards for Music Education adopted in the United States in 1994. A comprehensive music education for all children should include all of these goals. Realistically, goals are addressed in varying degrees at different age levels.

1. Singing
2. Playing instruments
3. Improvising
4. Composing and arranging
5. Reading and notating music
6. Listening to, analyzing, and describing music
7. Evaluating music and musical performances
8. Understanding relationships between music and other arts/other disciplines
9. Understanding music in relation to history and culture

Pages of the Parent's Guide coincide with the same-numbered pages in the student book. If your child is practicing songs on page 6, you can turn to page 6 in the Parent's Guide and find ways to review new concepts (introduced under the heading **What's New?**), and specific ways you can practice the new rhythms together. You might learn a few new things yourself!

In addition to specific activities that reinforce concepts and skills introduced on each page, look for other regular features throughout the guide:

What is .....? Explanations of words used in *Artistry in Strings*.
Did You Know? Interesting information relating to a song.

Practice Tips
- General ideas for getting the most out of practice time.

Be Creative!
Enrichment activities that foster a child's individual creativity and open the door to self expression.

Instrument Care
- Important reminders about keeping the instrument and bow in top playing condition.

This symbol is used to indicate when a song is included on the accompaniment compact discs. If the discs weren't attached to your child's book, you may purchase them separately (100F) from your music store. Practicing and performing with the accompaniment CDs is fun and rewarding!

UNIT I – Ready, Set, Go!

What is a *Swingercise*?
Swingercises are learning games. They take everyday (non-musical) skills and translate them into the specialized movements or skills of playing a string instrument. They are used to teach new techniques, as well as to review and refine techniques previously introduced. *Swingercises* are also good warm-up activities to use at the beginning of a practice session or lesson. Detailed photo sequences of each *Swingercise* are included in the student book, and will help your child remember how to practice each movement at home.

Bow Stroke Rhythms I – SwingStrum is introduced. Help your child practice the rhythm apart from the physical gesture, then do them at the same time.

1. Set a steady beat. To do this, turn on the metronome (mm = 60) or watch the tick of the second hand on a clock, and pat your thigh on each tick.
2. Speak word phrase A over and over to the beat: "Swing Strum rest, Swing Strum rest." There should be a natural accent (emphasis) on the first word of the phrase, "Swing," and a feeling of "1-2-3, 1-2-3."
3. Now, have your child do the graceful *Swingercise* gesture as you continue saying "Swing Strum rest." If the gesture seems too fast, reset the metronome to a slower beat.
4. Repeat the process using word phrase B: "Strum rest Swing, Strum rest Swing."
5. Together can you think of names of family members, pets, or places that could be substituted for "Swing Strum"?

Do you notice how relaxed the students look in the photos? They seem proud to work with their instruments, too. Your child will gain that same level of ease and confidence in no time.

MARK "ORCHESTRA DAYS" ON THE FAMILY CALENDAR. HELP YOUR CHILD REMEMBER TO BRING HER INSTRUMENT, MUSIC, AND OTHER ITEMS TO SCHOOL ON THOSE DAYS.

Practice Tip

- Help your child set up a regular time, and a good place, for practicing. Many young musicians choose to practice at the same time every day, like before school or right after dinner. The best place in your home for them to practice is a quiet place, away from the television, telephone, computer, and other disruptions. If possible, remain nearby to monitor and support your child's practicing.

Bow Stroke Rhythms II – Ups 'n' Downs

Again, help your child practice each rhythm pattern apart from the physical movements of "Down Bow" and "Up Bow."

1. Set a steady beat on the metronome or by watching the second hand of a clock.
2. Speak word phrase A over and over to the beat: "Down Up rest rest, Down Up rest rest." There should be a natural accent (emphasis) on the first word of the phrase, "Down," and a feeling of "1-2-3-4, 1-2-3-4."
3. Have your child pantomime the two bow directions, "Down" and "Up," as you continue saying "Down Up rest rest."
4. Repeat the process using word phrase B: "Down Up Down Up."
5. Instrument and bow to playing position? Now have your child play word phrase A on one of the open strings as you both say the words. Repeat the phrase several times as he plays the rhythm on other open strings. As the bow moves, watch that it stays parallel to the bridge.
6. Speak word phrase B as your child plays it on an open string. Keep the beat steady! Repeat this phrase several times, too, as he plays the rhythm on other open strings.
7. Another day play the echo game. You say the words of either word phrase A or B, and your child will echo your phrase on one of the open strings.

Practice Tips

- Using a music stand allows a musician to be able to sit or stand tall and hold the instrument correctly.
- Fingers, hands, and arms may tire easily because they are learning new movements and positions. If this happens, it's good to take a few seconds to shake out the hands and arms, or wiggle the fingers, to relax the muscles.

When students play with others they must listen not only to themselves, but also to the pitch, pulse, and mood created when all parts come together. A book of piano accompaniments is available for *Artistry in Strings* Book 1. It contains an accompaniment for every song in the book, beginning on page 6 with **1. Our First Bow Strokes**. Do you or another family member play piano? Students will have fun being accompanied by a family member, and at the same time, begin to develop their sense of ensemble.

Instrument Care

- String instruments and bows must be handled with care. Avoid letting someone other than your young musician play her instrument.

At the top of page 6, several notes, rests, and other music symbols are introduced under **What's New?**. Have your child point out at least two places where each new symbol is used in songs **1–10**. Can your child name the strings of the instrument, in order from lowest to highest? From highest to lowest? *(See* **What's New?** *for the correct answers.)*

Be Creative!
Give your child a piece of manuscript paper and have her copy each new note, rest, and symbol three times. It is important that the symbols look exactly like they do at the top of page 6. (Manuscript paper is available at your local music store, or you can photocopy page 62 in this guide.)

Songs **1–6** are based on **Bow Stroke Rhythms II – Ups 'n' Downs**.
Help your child practice each song as he did when **Bow Stroke Rhythms II** were introduced.
1. Set a steady beat.
2. Speak the rhythm of the song using the word phrase(s).
3. Pantomime the rhythm of the song with an imaginary bow while saying the word phrase(s).
4. Play the song on the correct open string(s) while saying the word phrase(s). As the bow moves, it should stay parallel to the bridge.

Which of the songs has a rhythm that does not match either "Down Up rest rest" or "Down Up Down Up" word phrase? *(5. G-ography)*

Look at **2. Bowing on A**. After your child has written in the counting, have her show you what it means to count and clap it aloud. Together count and clap songs **1–6**. Be sure each quarter note or quarter rest gets a number (1, 2, 3, or 4), depending on its place in the measure. Keep a steady beat!

Assessment in beginning orchestra?
In previous generations, if students were eager participants in orchestra (or band or choir) and didn't cause trouble, they could count on the "easy A" on their report card. That is no longer true. In today's beginning orchestra, it is common for teachers to assess their students' developing knowledge and playing skills in every lesson and every rehearsal. Assessments may be done informally, by listening to an entire section or group of students playing a given song, or more formally, with each student demonstrating a skill or playing a song individually. Sometimes students will be told ahead of time to be prepared to play a particular song, other times the teacher may want to check a certain skill "on the spot." Either way, the two most important reasons for a teacher to assess students individually are 1) to be able to provide specific feedback to each student, and 2) to guide the planning of future instruction.

If your young musician talks of an upcoming assessment or playing test, check the **Assessment Record** (distributed to students in class) for specific objectives the teacher will be watching and listening for. Help your child carry out enough careful repetitions to master the objectives and feel confident in her ability to play the song.

What is a Roundabout?
In a Roundabout, the student plays a single rhythm pattern on each string in succession from highest to lowest, or lowest to highest. You will notice there is a Roundabout whenever a new rhythm pattern or bow stroke is introduced throughout the book.

Bow Stroke Rhythms III – The Lunch Bunch
The rhythms get more interesting (and more fun to play) with the introduction of eighth notes. Use the now familiar process to help your child practice these new word phrases and rhythm patterns: Set, Speak, Pantomime, and Play. Songs **7–10** are based on **Bow Stroke Rhythms III – The Lunch Bunch**.

When your child is able to play songs **9** and **10** at a steady tempo it's time to add the CD accompaniment. Each song on the CD is played twice. The first time you will hear both the accompaniment and the student part; the second time only the accompaniment. Students will have fun playing with the wide variety of accompaniments on the CD, and at the same time, develop their sense of intonation, steady tempo, and ensemble.

Together listen to **9. What's for Lunch?**. Say the word phrases for the entire song as your child pantomimes with an imaginary bow, then restart the track and have her play along. Another day, listen to the accompaniment 2–3 times. What instruments do you hear? What feeling do you get from the music? Based on these impressions (and the title), talk about the type of food your family might be served if you heard this song as background music in a restaurant.

When your child is able to play **10. Leftovers** with the accompaniment, encourage her to memorize the song. Strategies for memorizing:

- Play the song several times, then play it without looking at the music.
- Sing the song using the word phrases, then close the book and play it.
- Listen to the CD, follow along in the music, and sing the melody. Close the book and sing the melody along with the CD, visualizing the music in your head. Listen again and play the song with the CD.

Your child's teacher may offer additional strategies to help students memorize music.

Be Creative!
Take out colored pencils matching the colors of the 4 strings and have your child fill in this line of squares below to create a song. What rhythm or pitch patterns might he make? *(A song may be easier to play if it moves between adjacent strings.)* Uncolored squares will mean "rest." As he plays the new song, names of the strings should be said quietly.

Bow Stroke Rhythms IV – Down Under

More new rhythm patterns! Take time again to Set, Speak, Pantomime, and Play.

- Another day play the echo game. You say the words of one of the word phrases, and your child will echo your phrase on the open strings.
- Together can you think of your own word phrases associated with Australia to match each rhythm pattern?

Songs **11–13** use **Bow Stroke Rhythms IV – Down Under**. Remind your child to speak the word phrase(s) as he plays each song.

Did You Know? Due to their isolated location, Australia and New Zealand are home to many unique species of wildlife. Kiwis, flightless birds with long slender beaks, are native to New Zealand. In Australia, there are about 45 different types of kangaroos. The largest kangaroos can cover a distance of 19 feet with each jump. Other wildlife unique to "The Land Down Under" includes koalas, wombats, and kookaburras.

When your child is able to play songs **12** and **13** at a steady tempo it's time to add the CD accompaniment.

First, listen to **12. Kiwi Birds and Kangaroos** 2–3 times, and imagine you are riding on the Skyrail Rain Forest Cableway between Cairns and Kuranda (in Australia). Talk about what you might see and hear as you ride across the top of the rain forest canopy. What in the music reminds you of those sights and sounds? Restart the track so your child can play along. You can help her stay with the accompaniment by saying the word phrases.

Listen to the count-off that sets the speed for **13. Kangaroos and Kiwi Birds**. Clap along to help internalize the pulse. Listen to the accompaniment again and clap the rhythm of the song, then say the word phrases as your child pantomimes with an imaginary bow. Restart the track and have her play along. Another day, talk about the wildlife species unique to Australia/New Zealand that comes to mind when listening to the music, and why.

Be Creative!
> Take out a piece of manuscript paper for your child to copy song **13**. Be sure the clef and time signature are at the beginning of the line. Neatness counts! Then on a new staff line, she can rewrite song **13**, but this time mix the measures into a different order. Play the new song with the CD accompaniment. Does it work?

After your child has completed the instructions given in the lesson book for **14. WriteRight Rhythms,** he is ready to add more pitches to the rhythm and make up a song. Say the word phrases, and encourage her to move between all 4 open strings. Play it again using a different order of strings. Play it fast, play it slow!

> "The child must repeat and repeat if he is to learn. Knowledge is not skill. Knowledge plus 10,000 times is skill."
> – Shinichi Suzuki

Before playing **16. The Lunch Bell,** ask your child to find the measure(s) in the song that use each word phrase rhythm:

- "Yum! Yum! Peanut Butter" | *measures 1, 3, 5, 6*
- "Pepperoni Pizza" | *measure 7*
- "Tom Took A Turkey Toe" | *not used*
- "Down Up Down Up" | *measures 2, 4*

What word phrase might be said for measure 8?

Listen to the count-off that sets the speed for **16. The Lunch Bell.** Clap along on the beat to help internalize the pulse. Listen again and clap the rhythm of the song. In which measures do you hear hand clapping as part of the accompaniment? *(1, 3, 5, 6)* As your child plays along, have her listen to see that the eighth notes she is playing are synchronized with the clapping on the CD.

When your child is able to play **16. The Lunch Bell** with the accompaniment, encourage her to memorize the song. (See <u>Strategies for Memorizing</u> on page 7 of this book.) He can be proud to play two songs from memory! Continue to play both songs frequently to be able to remember them easily.

17. The Lunch Bunch Down Under is a great song for reviewing all four of the open strings, and **Bow Stroke Rhythms III** and **IV**.

- See how fast your child can name all the pitches of part A in order, from left to right.
  Violin & Bass: A-A-A-A-D-A   D-D-G-G-G-D   A-E-E-A-A-A   D-D-G-G-G-G
  Viola & Cello: A-A-A-A-D-A   D-D-G-G-G-D   A-A-A-A-A-A   D-D-G-G-G-G

- Without looking at the lesson book, can your young musician draw the notes that represent the rhythm of these word phrases on a piece of manuscript paper?

  "Pepperoni Pizza" | *part A, measure 1*
  "Kangaroo In The Zoo" | *part A, measure 2*
  "Tom Took A Turkey Toe" | *part A, measure 3*
  "Yum! Yum! Peanut Butter" | *part A, measure 4*
  "Down Kiwi Up Kiwi" | *part B, measure 2*

- Have your child say the word phrases as he plays each part, A and B.

Instrument Care

- When your child is finished playing the instrument, she must always loosen the bow, and wipe any rosin from the bow stick and surface of the instrument with a soft cloth. Store the instrument and bow securely.

> **What are Harmonics?**
>
> The harmonics of stringed instruments are high tones with a somewhat light, transparent sound. These high tones are produced by lightly touching the string at certain places rather than pressing the string firmly to the fingerboard as is done with most pitches. Touching a string lightly at its half-way point will produce the harmonic an octave higher than the open string. One symbol used to indicate a note is to be played as a harmonic is a small circle above it with a finger indication.

18. The Magic Octave gives students practice playing harmonics. Help your child think through this song before playing it.

1. Touch the D-string lightly at the correct place and bow to play the harmonic.
2. Count and play the second and fourth measures of the song, the open D-string.
3. Count and play the first and third measures of the song, the D-string harmonics.
4. Slowly play the first 4 measures.
5. Repeat steps 1, 2, and 3 to play the B section on the G-string.
6. When your child can play the first 4 measures, and the last 4 measures, she is ready to play the song straight through.

Songs **19–22** use harmonics, too. You might approach these songs in the same way as recommended for **18. The Magic Octave**, easy as 1-2-3-4-5-6!

Listen to the count-off that sets the speed for **20. Open Air**. Clap along on the beat to help internalize the pulse, then restart the track and pantomime the position of the notes with the left hand. Add the bow and play the entire song. Another day, listen to the CD together. Talk about what percussion instrument might be appropriate to add, and why.

When your child is able to play **22. Hungry Harmonics**, listen to the accompaniment 2–3 times. Can you both hear how the student part fits in? Notice the "jazzy" vibraphone melody, too. Then it's time for your child to play along. Encourage her to memorize this song and continue to play it for fun!

Be Creative!

Your child can use **The Lunch Bunch** and **Down Under** rhythms to make up (improvise) her own combinations of open string and harmonic pitches. Then, play the echo game. You say one of the word phrases and your child will echo it using open string and harmonic pitches.

Continue to experiment (carefully)! What other new and interesting sounds can be made by bowing, plucking, strumming, or finger tapping on the instrument?

Now students are ready to begin to use the fingers of their left hand to play more pitches. Ask your child to show you where he was instructed to place the left hand in *Swingercise* #8. If he also plays piano, your child may have noticed fingers are numbered differently to play the string instrument.

In songs **23** and **24**, there are some horizontal lines placed above or below the notes telling students to leave down a given finger *(see page 11* **What's New?***)*. You can be the extra set of eyes to watch that your child continues to leave that finger down as long as indicated.

Listen to the count-off and clap the steady beat of **24. Octave Olympics**. Don't be fooled by the moving notes you hear — the beat is actually quite slow. Play along. Another day, listen again to the accompaniment. Talk about an Olympic sport (from the Summer or Winter Games) that comes to mind when you hear this music, and why.

Did You Know? The ancient Olympic Festival and Games was held every four years between 776 B.C. and 393 A.D. Male athletes from every Greek city-state competed for substantial riches and privileges. As early as the 5th and 4th centuries B.C., winning athletes were celebrated in odes (poems), sculpture, and commemorative coins. The modern Olympic Games were restarted in 1896 in Athens, and events for women were added in 1900. Nowadays, what prizes do the winners receive? In what ways are today's Olympic winners honored? Can you think of the only Olympic sport today in which men and women compete against each other as equals? *(Equestrian)*

Practice Tip

- Be sure there is time in each practice session to play some favorite songs and the ones that have been memorized. With or without the accompaniment, memorized or read from the book, it's fun to go back and review earlier songs. You and your child will be surprised at how much easier they now seem!
- Each day, review the teacher's feedback and instructions given on an assignment sheet, on the pages of the lesson book, and on the Assessment Record.

Be Creative!

On pages 9 through 11, have your child look for 6 (or more?) different pitches. Notice which note heads are on a line, and which are on a space. What is the letter name of each pitch? *(See* **What's New?** *on previous pages.)*

Give your child a piece of manuscript paper. For each pitch found on pages 9 through 11, have her draw 2 quarter notes and 1 pair of eighth notes, followed by a quarter rest. *(Not sure which is which? Look back to* **What's New?** *on page 6.)* Be sure that the notes drawn look exactly like the ones in the book. Is each stem going the correct direction, and on the correct side of each note head?

26. Pizza Pizzazz is a fun song to play, but it is also a bit tricky. Ask your child about the first note in measure 2 and the last note in measure 4. Are they the same? *(No. The D in measure 2 is fingered with the third finger on the A-string. The D in measure 4 is a harmonic, and played by lightly touching the halfway point of the D-string.)* Encourage her to practice slowly and carefully.

Listen a few times to the CD accompaniment for song **26. Pizza Pizzazz**, and talk about the differences you both hear between the first time through and the repeat. *(Hints: Do the same instruments play both times? Does the music get louder, softer, or stay the same? Are the same melodies and harmonies played both times?)* Another day, play along with the CD or someone playing the piano accompaniment.

When your child is able to play **26. Pizza Pizzazz** with the accompaniment, encourage her to memorize it. Strategies for memorizing this song:

- Study the first line of the song. Look for measures that are the same *(measures 1 and 3)*. Play the first line 5 times, each time thinking about the measures that are the same. Do the same with the second line.
- Compare lines 1 and 2. How are these lines similar?
- Listen to the CD and pantomime the song.
- Play the song several more times while looking at the music. Then, play it with the CD, without looking at the music.

Songs **27–29** are based on **Bow Stroke Rhythms V–The Sports Report**. Set, Speak, Pantomime, and Play A–E.

- How many beats are in each measure? *(3)*
- Another day play the echo game. You say the words of one of the word phrases, and have your child echo your phrase on the open strings.
- Together can you think of your own sports-related word phrases to match each rhythm pattern?

Recital Time!

Your young artist has reached the end of Unit I, a milestone! Suggest she play a short recital for the family. Keep this event very low key. (It might even take place when one or more rival siblings are away.) Her program might include some of the memorized songs, other favorites, and maybe even an original composition or two (from the WriteRight Worksheet assignments given by the orchestra teacher). Prompt your child to introduce the name of each song before playing it. At the conclusion of each song, encourage her to look at you (the audience) and smile and nod to accept your applause.

If you have a video camera, start a new tape of your child's work. Record this casual recital, and afterwards, watch the tape with your child. Ask for her reflections in each area:

- Posture?
- Was the bow parallel to the bridge?
- Which song did he like best, and why?
- Who might she play for next?

UNIT II – The D-String

At the top of page 13, several terms and symbols, a rest, and new notes on the D-string are introduced under **What's New?**. Can your child find at least one place where each new symbol is used in songs 30–32? *(The natural sign is first used in song 35 on page 14.)*

Have your child show you where fingers should be placed on the D-string to play each note. Compare his finger placement to the photos in the student book.

What is a half step?
The smallest distance (interval) between two pitches in music of western European traditions is a half step. Notice how half steps are marked on the diagram in the book.

What is a whole step?
A whole step is the interval between two pitches equal to two half steps.

Ask your child which of the following pairs of notes are half steps and which are whole steps. He may look at the fingerboard drawings on page 13 for help.

E to F *(half step)*   G to F *(whole step)*
E to F♯ *(whole step)*   F♯ to E *(whole step)*
F♯ to G *(half step)*   F to E *(half step)*
F to G *(whole step)*   E to D *(whole step)*
G to F♯ *(half step)*

What is a Down 'n' Back Variations song?
In a Down 'n' Back Variations song, the student repeats a rhythm on each pitch of a finger pattern. You will notice a Down 'n' Back or Up 'n' Back Variations whenever a new finger pattern is introduced.

Have your child play **30. Down 'n' Back Variations** five times today, each time using a different **Sports Report** rhythm.

Name the notes of **32. Steps to Success** in rhythm before playing. A sharp sign remains in effect through the end of a measure. *(In measure 3, the notes are G-F♯-E-F♯.)*

 As your child plays with the CD, encourage him to match the confident, relaxed feeling of the music.

Practice Tip

- Your child's fingernails must be short if he is going to be able to press the strings firmly to the fingerboard.

Songs **33–38** on page 14 give students more practice playing D-string finger patterns, and recognizing differences between F-sharp and F-natural. With your child listen to the accompaniment CD for **33. Country Walk**, and sing the melody using the syllable "lah." Notice the sound of the F-sharps. Listen to **38. Hotaru Koi** on the CD, too, and sing the melody using "lah." Notice that the sound of the F-naturals is slightly, but importantly, different from the sound of the F-sharps.

Each day before your child plays songs **33–38**, have him prepare by doing one of the following:

- Set a steady beat. Say the names of the pitches in rhythm; say "rest" for each rest.
- Clap and count the rhythm of the song. Check the time signature and watch out for the rests!
- Finger the Left Hand while saying the pitches. Where are the half steps? *(Half steps are G to F♯, and E to F.)*
- Finger the Left Hand while saying the counting. Play it!

Music often suggests a visual image to its performers and listeners. Together consider the image you get from the title and sound of each of these songs.

33. What might someone see and feel on a walk in the country? Listen to the CD for clues. Can you convey the same feeling through the music?

34. Do you think the composer had a figure skater or hockey player in mind when this song was titled? What clues does the music give to help you answer this question? Also, memorize **34. The Ice Skater's Minuet** to play for fun and for others. Can you find a pattern in the notes that will help you memorize it? *(The middle note in most measures is D.)*

Once your child has written the counting, drawn the bar lines, and clapped and counted the rhythm, he is ready to play **36. The All-Sports Event**. When playing this song with the CD, encourage him to match the confident and energetic feeling of the accompaniment.

38. Hotaru Koi is a Japanese folk song. Find Japan on the world map located in the student book. Together listen to the accompaniment. Do you hear an instrument that sounds like the shakuhachi (bamboo flute)? Have your child think of a word that describes the mood of this song, then match it as he plays along with the CD. Also, have him memorize this song for another recital at the end of Unit II.

Be Creative!

Challenge your child to play **38. Hotaru Koi** as if it were a song about elephants rather than fireflies. Would it sound different if it were a song about tigers? If so, how?

Bow Stroke Rhythms VII – Slow Bow

More new rhythm patterns! Take time again to Set, Speak, Pantomime, and Play rhythms A–C on an open string.

In **39. Slow Bow Roundabout**, select a pattern (A, B, or C) and play it on the open strings in the order given. Speak the word phrase as your child plays to be sure the half note sounds for 2 beats. Don't forget the rests!

Songs **40–42** use **Bow Stroke Rhythms VII – Slow Bow**. Remind your child to say these word phrase(s) as he plays each song. What can be said for measures with 4 quarter notes? *("1-2-3-4" or "Bow-ing Bow-ing." "Down Up Down Up" used earlier also works except in* **41. Midland Meadows***, measure 7, where "Up Down Up Down" matches the direction of the bow.)*

- Another day, study part A of **41. Midland Meadows**. The A part is made up of two phrases, measures 1–4 and 5–8. A phrase is a set of notes that form a musical idea, much like words form a sentence. Compare the pitches and rhythms of the second phrase (measures 5–8) to those of the first phrase (measures 1–4). You will discover the phrases are exactly the same with one exception. What is it? *(The rhythm in measure 3 is different from measure 7.)*

- Compare the 2 phrases of part B, measures 1–4 and 5–8. You will discover these phrases are exactly the same, with one exception. What is it? *(The pitches and rhythms in measures 3 and 7 are not the same.)* Use your knowledge of the phrases, and their similarities and differences, to practice more efficiently.

Find England and France on the world map in the student book (page 56).

Did You Know? You can travel by train between London and Paris in about 3 hours. The trip will take you through the Chunnel, a 23 mile tunnel built under the English Channel. The Chunnel opened in 1994, and cost $15 billion to build. The idea of a tunnel under the English Channel was first considered in 1802.

Notice the new time signature in **43. Snake Charmer**. Together say the counting before your child plays this song. Because the time signature is 2/4, count no higher than "1-2."

Have your child clap the steady pulse of the count-off to help feel the speed, then restart the track to play along. Encourage him to match the smooth, snake-like style of the accompaniment. This is another good solo to memorize!

Instrument Care

- Keep a record of the instrument's serial number with your other important papers. (To find the serial number, look inside the f-holes.) Be sure the instrument is covered by your homeowner's insurance.

16

No new skills or symbols are introduced on this page, just 6 new songs to play! Have your child study the songs. In which one will he play F-naturals? *(46. Sharps & Naturals.)* How is F-natural fingered? *(See D-string finger patterns on page 13.)*

Find Norway on the world map in the student book.

With your child, listen to **44. Frida's Favorite Fjord**, and sing the melody on "lah." Notice the sound of the F-sharps. Continue to practice this song without the accompaniment, and pay special attention to the F-sharps and "Slow Bow" half notes. Listen again another day. What types of steps might people use to dance to this song? *(Possible answers might include: Small, Large, Light, Heavy, Hop, Leap, Stomp, Glide, and/or Twirl.)*

Practice Tip

- As you listen to your child practice, do you hear a hesitation or mistake? Encourage your child to practice the difficult measure or measures over and over until he can play them correctly. Then, play the song all the way through.

Look and listen carefully as your child plays **46. Sharps & Naturals**:

- E to F-natural is a half step. These notes are found in measures 5 and 7 of the A part, and measures 2 and 4 of the B part.
- E to F-sharp is a whole step. These notes are found in measures 1 and 3 of the A part, and measures 6 and 8 of the B part.
- Young players often let their notes extend into the rests. There should be no sound on the quarter rests.

Find Germany on the world map.

> **Did You Know?** World famous cuckoo clocks come from the Black Forest region of southwest Germany.

Together study **48. Cuckoo**. Compare the pitches and rhythms of the first phrase (measures 1–4) to those of the second phrase (measures 5–8). You will discover the phrases are exactly the same, with one exception. What is it? *(The last pitch of each phrase is different.)* The third phrase (measures 9–12) is completely different from the first phrases. Is the final phrase more like the second or third phrase? *(2nd)* This knowledge of the similarities and differences helps musicians understand how the music is composed, and aids in memorizing.

Before playing **48. Cuckoo** with the CD, listen for the sound of cuckoo on the recording. Another day, listen again for the phrases that are similar, and the third phrase that is different, then play along from memory.

Be Creative!

Have your child experiment to create the song of another bird, or the sound of an animal, on his instrument. What symbol might be used to represent the sound?

> **Did You Know? Bile 'em Cabbage Down** is an American fiddle song. American fiddling has its roots in folk fiddling traditions of various European cultures (Irish, Scottish, Norwegian, etc.) Traditionally, these songs have been passed along by ear from fiddler to fiddler, though much of the music has, by now, been written down. Part of the fun in listening to fiddle music is that every fiddler has his or her own variation of the tune.

Visit the public library and borrow some recordings of fiddle music. You may be able to find a longer version of **Bile 'em Cabbage Down**, plus many other fun tunes!

Together listen to **49** and clap and count the rhythm of the melody *(1-&-2-& 1-2)*. Restart the track and have your child play along. Another day, listen again and describe the differences you hear between the first time through and the repeat.

On page 17 students are introduced to two new skills, Left Hand pizzicato and bow lift. Have your child show you how to do Left Hand pizzicato before playing **51. Arcato**.

- "Arcato" isn't a musical term, but it describes what's happening in this song. Can your child figure out from which two words "arcato" has been created, and what those words mean? *(Arco means bow, and pizzicato means pluck the string.)*
- Watch out for the rhythms in measures 3 and 7. *(You might combine two of the rhythms from* **Bow Stroke IV – Down Under** *and say "Kan-ga-roo Up Ki-wi.")*

Have your child show you how to do the bow lift before playing the first two measures of **52. Hot Cross Buns**.

- If your child plays this song as written, with F-sharps, the interval between E and F-sharp is a whole step.
- Have him play the song again, but play all of the F-sharps as F-naturals. E to F-natural is a half step. You both should be able to hear that the song sounds different when F-naturals are played.
- Does your local bakery sell hot cross buns, or do you have a recipe to make them? It might be fun to serve them in the next week or so, and have your child perform the song for the rest of the family.

As your child is marking the half steps for **53. Shepherd's Hey**, you can help check his work by remembering:

- A sharp sign lasts for the entire measure. In measures 1, 3, and 5, the notes are F♯-G-A-F♯.
- F♯ to G is a half step. The interval between the first two notes of the song is a half step, as is the distance between the fourth and fifth notes of the song, and so on.

As your child plays **54. Loco Motive** with the CD, have him synchronize the eighth notes with the steady chugging of the train. Have him repeat the song several times, being aware of similar measures and patterns. It will be memorized in no time!

18

Quick Check! Have your child find an example of each symbol on pages 18–19.
- sharp *(measure 3, song 56)*
- harmonic *(last note, song 57)*
- Right Hand pizzicato *(song 61)*
- Left Hand pizzicato *(song 55)*
- bow lift *(measure 4, song 56)*
- 3 beats per measure *(song 56)*
- 4 beats per measure *(song 55)*
- 2 beats per measure *(song 61)*
- clef *(first symbol at the beginning of each staff)*
- bar line *(vertical lines that divide notes into measures)*
- measure *(between two bar lines)*
- repeat sign *(two dots next to the double bar line at the end of a song)*

Before your child plays songs **55** and **56**, have him say the names of the pitches. Do this several times so he can recite them without hesitation. *(Song **55** uses only the 4 open strings. Look on student book page 6 for the names of the open strings. Song **56** adds E, F♯, and G. Look on student book page 13 to be able to check the names of those pitches.)*

Did You Know? "Little Red Riding Hood," "Hansel and Gretel," and "Snow White and the Seven Dwarfs" are German folk tales.

As your child is learning **57. Du, Papa**, it should be played very slowly. He has a lot of things to be thinking about—D-string finger pattern with F-sharps, bow lifts, LH pizzicato, harmonics. Together compare the second line to the first line. Do you notice that both lines start out exactly the same way? Measure 14 is the same as which two measures? *(Measures 4 and 12.)*

Together listen to **57. Du, Papa**. Can you identify some of the instruments playing in this German band? Another day, listen to the count-off and clap along to help internalize the pulse. Restart the track and have your child play with the accompaniment.

Did You Know? Italian composer Guiseppe Verdi (1813–1901) enjoyed a long and successful career. He is best remembered for his serious, gloomy, and often violent operas, but he also composed several choral pieces. "Il Trovatore," from which the "Anvil Chorus" comes, was first performed in 1853.

As your child practices **58**, watch that his left elbow swings to the new string. Then have him join the "Anvil Chorus" on the accompaniment CD. Synchronize the pizzicato notes with the alternating anvil and crash cymbals.

Be Creative!

Take out a piece of manuscript paper for your child to copy song **59**. Be sure the clef and time signature are at the beginning of the first line (but only the clef at the beginning of subsequent lines). Neatness counts! Then on a new staff line, have him rewrite song **59**, substituting a quarter rest for one quarter note in each of the "piz-zi-ca-to" measures. Play the new song with a steady beat, then try it with the CD.

Songs **60–62** use octaves in their melodies. An octave is the interval (distance) between a note and the next lowest or highest note with the same name. The first two notes in **60. Octowaves** form an octave D to D. Challenge your child to find other octaves in these songs:

- **60. Octowaves** *(D to D in measures 2, 3, 4, 5, 6, 7. G to G in measures 1 and 7.)*
- **61. Pizzicato March** *(Look at the combination of both A and B parts to find G to G octaves in measures 1, 2, 3, 5, 8.)*
- **62. Octonics** *(G to G to G in measures 2–3 including the harmonic note, G to G in measure 8, and 8 repeating back to the beginning. D to harmonic D in 5–6.)*

Your child should play each song slowly at first, then a bit faster. It is important that the octave intervals "match," that is, sound in tune.

Did You Know? Antonín Dvořák was born in a small village in the country now known as the Czech Republic. In 1892, he moved to New York to become the director of the National Conservatory of Music. While he was living in America, he composed Symphony No. 9 ("From the New World") and "The American" string quartet. Today, these are two of his most well-known works.

Borrow a recording of Dvořák's entire Symphony No. 9 from the library, or purchase a CD from a local retailer or online. Can you determine the movement from which **63** was taken?

Another Quick Check! As your child plays song **63**, watch his technique.

- Left hand fingers stay down, as indicated, as he crosses strings.
- Right hand holds the bow correctly.
- Instrument is held correctly.
- Bow moves parallel to the bridge (perpendicular to the strings).

Encourage your child to follow the directions in the student book to complete **64. WriteRight Rhythms**. *(The highest number used when writing in the counting is "2" because the line has a $\frac{2}{4}$ time signature.)*

Be Creative!

Have your child play **64. WriteRight Rhythms** on the note D. Play **64** again using two notes of the D-string finger pattern to improvise a song. Remember, to "improvise" means to make up a melody as it's being played — whatever comes to mind. Another day, suggest he use three notes of the D-string finger pattern to improvise a new song, and then three different notes.

> **Did You Know?** "Mary Had a Little Lamb" was a poem by Mrs. Sarah J. Hale, published in 1830. It became the song we know today when, in 1868, the poem was set to a melody known as "Merrily We Roll Along."

As your child practices **65. Mary's Ba-a-ad Adventure**, he should be careful to play the first and third lines with F-sharp, and the middle line with F-natural. When he can play the entire song with a steady beat, suggest one of these additional activities to enrich the experience, and make practicing more fun!

- Change the rhythm of the song to accommodate a new verse, such as "A-ber-crom-bie had a ve-ry big snake." Have your child say the new words as he plays it. Together can you think of other zany verses?

Listen to **65** on the CD. Talk about how the music changes to let listeners know Mary's lamb is lost and then found. Another day, listen to the count-off and clap along to help internalize the pulse. Restart the track and have your child play with the accompaniment. Listen again to the CD. Imagine you are painters, and want to represent each part of the song with a color. What color would you choose for measures 1–8? Measures 9–16? Measures 17–24, and why?

With your child, listen to the accompaniment for **66. Seriously Slavic**, and sing the melody using the syllable "lah." Notice the sound of the F-naturals. E to F-natural is a half step. Can your child remember the three Sports Report rhythm phrases used in **66**? ("Vol-ley-ball," "Kim likes to swim," and "Fast run.")

Find Egypt on the world map in the student book.

> **Did You Know?** Cairo is the capital city of Egypt. It is located on the mighty Nile River. Giza, a suburb of Cairo, is the site of the Great Pyramids and the Great Sphinx.

Have your child play **67. Olive Chant** with the CD. Encourage him to use the full length of the bow to play smoothly. This is another good song for him to memorize and be able to play for others.

Students must write in the missing notes before playing **68. Jingle Bells**.

- You might suggest to your child that he begin by writing the lyrics under the melody line.
- Next, have him slowly sing the song, and think about the pitches — sometimes they repeat, and sometimes they move by steps or skips. Draw the note heads on the staff where they seem to go, then check his work by playing the notes on the instrument. Make changes as needed.
- Add the stems and beams to the note heads to write the rhythm. Check to be sure the rhythms in each measure add up to two full beats, and not more than that.
- While your child plays song **68**, you can add some "jingle" by shaking your keys.

69. Mean Green Halloween gives students a chance to use some of the interesting sounds they have (carefully!) created by bowing, plucking, strumming, string polishing, or finger tapping on their instrument. Encourage your child to practice each sound individually before putting them together to tell his tale.

Here's a very different poem in which to use some of those interesting sounds! Have your child read each verse and plan an appropriate sound effect on his instrument. Then, have him accompany your reading of "The Playground."

The Playground

There's a playground — check it out!
Race to the swing, begin to rise,
Swing high, swing low! Look at me!

Over there! Climb the ladder to the top,
Jostle across the suspension bridge,
Make it bounce, make it creak. This is fun!

Can't stop here!
Crawl through the tube,
Around the bend, reach the end.

Look out belo-o-o-ow!
Hold on and slide down the ten foot pole.
Thud!

Together study the A and B parts for **70. Lightly Row**. In five measures of the song the A and B parts play the same pitch at the same time. Can you find these places? *(Measures 3 – beat 2; 9 – all; 10 – beat 2; 11 – all; and 12 – beat 2.)*

Recital Time!

Your young artist has reached the end of Unit II, another milestone! Suggest he play a short recital again for the family. His program might include some of the memorized songs, other favorites, and an original composition from Unit II. Could you or another family member play the piano accompaniments?

Prompt your child to introduce the name of each song, along with the name of the composer or its country of origin. At the conclusion of each song, encourage him to look at the audience and smile and nod to accept their applause.

Record this performance on video tape. Afterwards, watch the tape together and talk about:

- Which songs were played accurately?
- Did he stay with the accompaniment?
- Which songs did the audience like best?
- Did he look poised and confident?

UNIT III – The A- and G-Strings

At the top of page 22, the dotted half note and new notes on the A-string are introduced under **What's New?**.

Have your child show you where fingers should be placed on the A-string to play each note. Compare her finger placement to the photos in the student book.

Ask your child which of the following pairs of notes are half steps and which are whole steps. She may look at the fingerboard drawings on page 22 for help.

    B to C *(half step)*   D to C *(whole step)*
    B to C♯ *(whole step)*   C♯ to B *(whole step)*
    C♯ to D *(half step)*   C to B *(half step)*
    C to D *(whole step)*   B to A *(whole step)*
    D to C♯ *(half step)*

Have your child play **72. Down 'n' Back Variations** five times today, each time using a different **Sports Report** rhythm. Another day, have her play **72** using the Slower Bow rhythm, and a Meter Melt. Watch that the bow remains parallel to the bridge as it moves (or perpendicular to the strings).

Take a good look at **73. The Escalator Song**—it starts on an up bow. Will the song end on a down bow or up bow? *(Down bow.)*

Before listening to the CD, anticipate the mood of the music. What do you think it might be—Serious, Light-hearted, Fun, Gentle, Anxious, Lonely, Enthusiastic, or something else? What instruments do you think the composer used to help convey the mood? Once you've answered these questions, listen to the CD. Were your guesses accurate? Listen again to catch the mood, and play along.

Bowing the first phrase (measures 1–4) of **74. Two Hills and a Valley** requires planning.

- Students should start the down bow for the first note at the frog.
- The second note will be an up bow played in the middle of the bow.
- The third note will be another down bow that ends near the tip of the bow.
- The dotted half note, then, can be played starting at the tip and there will be plenty of bow to make the note last for 3 beats.

Play **74. Two Hills and a Valley** with the CD. Another day, imagine you are riding on a train that is crossing the valley between two hills. Based on the feeling you get from the recording, what season might it be, and why? Have your child play this song several times with the CD, then play it without looking at their music. She will have it memorized in no time.

Encourage your child to use long, smooth bow strokes to play **75. Steak and Kidney Pie**. She should be thinking "Slow Bow" or "1-2" on the half notes so they are held for full value.

Be Creative!
Take out a piece of manuscript paper. It's time to play "The Disappearing A" game! Have your child copy **76. Brigadier's Brigade**, but substitute a quarter rest for each quarter note or pair of eighth notes on A. Can she play the new song with a steady beat?

Have your child play **77. Up 'n' Back Variations** five times today, each time using a different **Sports Report** rhythm. Watch out for the C-naturals. Compare her finger placement to the photo on page 22. Another day, have her play **77** using the Slower Bow rhythm, and a Meter Melt.

Songs **78. Sports in Review** and **79. Mary's Minor Mirror** also have C-naturals. The interval between B and C-natural is a half step.

Once your child has written the counting, drawn the bar lines, and clapped and counted the rhythm, she is ready to play **78**. When playing this song with the CD, encourage her to play with energy and excitement. Keep the bow moving.

Practice Tip
- At the end of each practice session, your child should be able to answer two questions, "What improved today?" and "Which songs or skills need work?"

Caution! **80. Half-Step Mixerfixer** uses both C-sharp and C-natural. Have your child listen carefully to the CD. Be sure her pitches (and beats of silence) match those on the recording.

In **81. Cuban Sports Report**, what is played, C-sharp or C-natural, or both? *(Only C-sharp. Since a sharp sign lasts for the entire measure, all of the Cs in measure 7 are C-sharp.)* Have your child play along with the CD. Listen to the accompaniment and name the percussion instruments you hear. The next day have her play **81** with the piano accompaniment.

Be Creative!
After she has completed **82. WriteRight Rhythms**, have your child play the line on the note A. Play **82** again using two notes of the A-string finger pattern to improvise a song. Another day, suggest she use three notes of the A-string finger pattern to improvise a new song, and then three different notes.

Key signatures are introduced on this page. Until now, students have been used to seeing an occasional sharp sign next to pitches in a song. When using a key signature, however, sharps are given at the beginning of each staff, and it is up to the player to remember to use them throughout the song. The G Major Key Signature always has F-sharp. The D Major Key Signature always has F-sharp and C-sharp, written in that order.

Before playing **83. D Major Scale**, have your child look at the key signature and name the two sharps. The D Major Scale always uses F-sharp and C-sharp. Notice how the D Major Scale looks on the fingerboard diagram at the top of page 24 in the student book. Where are the half steps? *(Between F♯ and G, and C♯ and D.)* Circle the notes affected by the sharps.

Listen to the CD, and have your child "finger" along — set her fingers on the string as if to play the notes, but without making a sound. Turn off the CD, and have her continue to practice by fingering the notes of the left hand and playing pizzicato. When she can finger the scale easily, add the bow to play the rhythm. Within a few days, she will be ready to play along with the CD accompaniment.

Songs **84–86** are based on the notes of the D major scale.

Did You Know? The note D is the home tone — resting tone, tonic, "do" — of the D major scale and key signature. The final note of a melody in D major will most likely be the tonic D.

Bowing **84. Chanson Populaire Française** requires planning. At the end of measure 3, your child's bow must be at the tip so she has an entire up bow with which to play the dotted half note in measure 4. This bowing pattern repeats with every phrase of the song.

84 is a good song to memorize. It will be easier to do so if your child looks for patterns in both the rhythm and melody. *(Notice each phrase is always 3 measures of quarter notes followed by a dotted half note. Measures 9–11 are the same, and measures 13–15 are the same.)*

Have your child listen to **85. Beautiful Bohemia** on the CD and finger along, before actually playing the song. Notice that the glockenspiel is playing her part.

After your child is able to play **86. Skippin' the Scale** with the CD, she is ready to play "The Disappearing D" game. Today, continue to play with the CD, but substitute rests for all the Ds (both octaves). Another day, she can play all of the Ds and rest on the other pitches.

Practice Tip

- A second set of ears often hears different elements of a performance. Encourage your spouse or another significant adult to participate in your child's practice sessions, too.

Have your child show you how to follow music with 1st & 2nd endings.

Every song on page 25 begins with a pick-up note or notes. If your child is writing in the counting for each song:
- **87. Zeg Moeder, Waar Is Jan?**, the folk song from the Netherlands, begins on count 2.
- **88. There's Music in the Air** begins on count 4.
- The pick-up eighth notes in **89. Pick-Up a Turkey Toe** are counted "4-&".
- **90. Sweet Betsy from Pike** begins on count 3.

Look at the last measure of each song on this page, too.
- The last measure of **88**, and of **89**, have only 3 counts. Count 4 is found at the beginning of these songs as a pick-up note.
- The last measure of **87** has only 1 count. Where is count 2?
- The last measure of **90** has only 2 counts. Where is count 3?

Songs **87** and **88** are based on the notes of the G major scale.

> **Did You Know?** The note G is the home tone — resting tone, tonic, "do" — of the G major scale and key signature. The final note of a melody in G major will most likely be the tonic G. The G major scale and key signature always have F-sharp.

Practice Tip

- Before playing a new song for the first time, check the key signature, the time signature, look for measures with unusual rhythms or complicated note patterns, check the speed, and check for specific bowings.

Find the Netherlands on the world map in the student book.

> **Did You Know?** The Netherlands is the delta of Europe. Here the Rhine, Maas, and Schelde Rivers empty into the North Sea. A large system of dikes and dams protects nearly half of the land from being flooded. Since the 1500s, windmills have also been used to pump water from the lowlands and keep them dry.

Before playing with the CD, listen to **87. Zeg Moeder, Waar is Jan?**. Notice the light-hearted mood of the music. Can you and your child hear that the tuba plays on count 1 of each measure? Listen to the count-off then join in!

In songs **89** and **90**, ask your child if she will play C-natural or C-sharp. *(C-sharp, according to the D major key signature.)*

As you listen to the accompaniment CD for **89** and **90**, have your child think of a word that describes the different mood of each song, then match it as she plays along. **Pick-Up a Turkey Toe** would be a fun song to memorize and have as part of her repertoire!

Watch that your child begins **89** on a down bow, not an up bow.

Students are learning new bow stroke styles on this page, martelé (short and crisp sounds) and legato (smooth sounds). Have your child demonstrate both styles for you. Can you hear the difference between them?

Have your child practice the martelé stroke on song **91**. She will start this Meter Melt by playing 4 quarter notes in each measure. Then, repeat the song with 3 quarter notes per measure, then 2, then 1. You can be the extra set of ears and listen for the pop!

As your child plays **93. Martelé Olé!** with the CD, encourage her to listen to the steady eighth notes of the xylophone and maracas. This will help her maintain the steady pulse, and not rush through the rests. Another day, listen for the cheerful violin countermelody that joins in on the repeat.

Has your child reached a plateau?
After a few months of study it is not uncommon for the excitement and newness of playing a string instrument to begin to wear off. Skills become more complex, and progress may slow. It's especially important at times like this that your young artist receive your support and encouragement!

Helpful Hints:
1. Continue to take an active role in her practice sessions. Some days that might mean listening from a nearby room and commenting, "I liked that song you just played, could you play it again?" Other days you might be sitting beside your child helping to catch a hesitation in a song, correct a fingering, or talking about what you both hear on the accompaniment CD.
2. Let your child know you are proud her accomplishments in music, as well as in other areas. Remember, actions often speak louder than words.
3. Watch the video tape of the recitals at the end of Units I and II. Acknowledge and celebrate! the progress she has made.
4. Friends can join together and make practice sessions more enjoyable.
5. Take the entire family to an orchestra performance.
6. Listen to recorded orchestral music. You might check out some CDs from the public library, listen to a classical FM station such as National Public Radio, or purchase recordings for your own family collection.
7. If she feels comfortable doing so, look for opportunities for your young artist to perform for others. It is particularly important that students feel prepared and successful in their early performances.

Instrument Care
- When the practice or rehearsal is finished, loosen the bow, and wipe any rosin from the bow stick and surface of the instrument with a soft, dry cloth. Store the instrument and bow securely.

More opportunities to practice martelé and legato styles, playing in the keys of G major and D major, pick-up notes, 1st & 2nd endings, harmonics, and D-string and A-string finger patterns.

94. Arpeggio Joe is based on only 3 chords. Individual notes can be displaced an octave higher or lower in an arpeggio without changing the chord.
- Measures 1, 2, and 7–8: D chord (D-F♯-A).
- Measures 3 and 4: G chord (G-B-D).
- Measures 5 and 6: A chord (A-C♯-E).

In the student book it says to play **94. Arpeggio Joe** three different ways—first legato, then pizzicato, then martelé. Listen to the CD together. Can you name the bowing style of the notes on the recording? *(Martelé)* Play along with the CD and match the bowing style. Play the song two more times to use legato, then pizzicato. Another day, listen to the song on the CD, and name some percussion instruments that might be added to the accompaniment.

Study the first line of **95. Onward, Upward**. Spell the chord that is used in the melody of the first line. *(D-F♯-A)* Study the notes used in **97. The Race Track**, too, and spell the chord. *(G-B-D)*

Practice Tip

- Be sure there is time in each practice session to play some favorite songs and the ones that have been memorized. With or without the accompaniment, memorized or read from the book, it's fun to go back and review earlier songs.

What is the name of the key signature used in **96. Crispy Icicles**? *(G Major)*

As your child plays **96** with the CD, encourage her to synchronize the quarter notes of the melody with the steady rhythm of the sleigh bells in the accompaniment. Another day, listen carefully to the bowing styles used on the CD. Can you hear the difference between the martelé at the beginning, and legato style in measure 4?

Before playing **98. Pick-Up Strings** with the CD, have your child listen carefully to the bowing style played by the violin. Is the style legato or martelé? *(Legato)* When your child is ready to join the "jazzy" accompaniment, caution her to count and play steady quarter notes as written in the book. For fun, she could play this piece pizzicato.

The first measure of **99. Pop! Goes the Bubble Wrap** is played martelé. In what bowing style should the other measures be played, and how do you know? *(Simile means continue to play in the same way, so the rest of the song should be played martelé.)*

At the top of page 28, the Flat ♭ and new notes on the G-string are introduced under **What's New?**.

Have your child show you where fingers should be placed on the G-string to play each note. Compare her finger placement to the photos in the student book.

Ask your child which of the following pairs of notes are half steps and which are whole steps. She may look at the fingerboard drawings on page 28 for help.

A to B♭ *(half step)*	B♭ to C *(whole step)*	C to B♭ *(whole step)*
A to B *(whole step)*	C to B *(half step)*	B to A *(whole step)*
B to C *(half step)*	B♭ to A *(half step)*	A to G *(whole step)*

Have your child play each half of **100. Down 'n' Down, Up 'n' Up** slowly. Be the extra set of eyes to watch that the finger is placed correctly to differentiate between B-natural and B-flat.

Study **101. Major Gee's Waltz**. What is the name of the key? *(G Major)* How many beats are in each measure? *(3)* If your child lightly circles (with a pencil, never pen) the first note in each measure, she will have a G major scale. Have her play the G major scale on dotted half notes, 3 beats per pitch.

Together listen to song **101** on the CD. There is a light, jazzy quality to it. Based on the sound of the music, think about the kind of character Major Gee could be. What might he or she look like? Is "Major" a name or title? Where might you hear **Major Gee's Waltz** being played? When your child has developed an image of Major Gee, she is ready to play along with the CD. Encourage her to keep "Major Gee" in mind as the waltz is played, and memorize the solo for future performances.

Study **102. Half-Step Mixerfixer**. When a flat is written next to a note, it remains in effect for the rest of the measure, or until a natural sign cancels the flat. How many B-flats are in measure 3? *(2)* In measure 6? *(2)*

- See how fast your child can read the pitches in this song in order, from left to right.

  C-B-C   C-B♭-C   B♭-A-B♭   B-A-G   G-A-G-A   B♭-A-B♭-B   G-A-B♭-B   C-B-C

- Encourage your child to practice this song slowly to be able to play all of the notes accurately.

Listen a few times to the accompaniment for song **102**, and talk about the differences you both hear between the first time through and the repeat. *(Hints: Do the same instruments play both times? Does the music get louder, softer, or stay the same?)* Another day, encourage your child to play along with the CD, matching the mood of the music.

100X

No new skills or symbols are introduced on this page, just 6 new songs to play! Remind your child to check the key signature and look for accidentals before beginning each song. Watch that the bow stays parallel to the bridge (or perpendicular to the strings).

Did You Know? Johann Sebastian Bach came from a very famous family of musicians. He was a teacher, master organist, and composer. He wrote vocal and instrumental music for many purposes, including keyboard exercises, chamber music, and pieces for church services. A popular instrument of Bach's time was the harpsichord. It looked a lot like a small grand piano, but the tone was very different. When the keys were pressed, its strings were plucked by quills to produce a soft, pizzicato-like tone.

Remind your child to play close attention to the B-flats as she plays **103. Minuet**. Notice, too, that the first two measures of each phrase (measures 1–2 and 5–6) are identical. Have your child memorize this song.

Together listen to **Minuet** on the CD. The accompaniment has the sound of a harpsichord. Listen to the song a second time and notice the extra little notes that "decorate" the melody.

Name the notes carefully in song **104. Three on Three in Three**. Your child should find 5 B-naturals, 1 B-flat, 1 F-sharp, 1 F-natural, 1 C-sharp, and 1 C-natural.

Help your child find three different chords in **105. Arpeggioller Coaster**:

- Measures 1, 2, 5, and 8: G chord (G-B-D).
- Measures 3, 4, and 7: D chord (D-F♯-A).
- Measure 6: C chord (C-E-G).

As the accompaniment begins, imagine you are both getting into the car of a roller coaster. What happens next as the music progresses? Does the music remind you of a roller coaster you've ridden before? Tomorrow play along.

Be Creative!

Take out a piece of manuscript paper. Have your child copy **105. Arpeggioller Coaster**, but change one quarter note in each measure into a pair of eighth notes or a quarter rest. Play the new song with the accompaniment CD.

Together study the A and B parts for **106. The Magic Mirror**. Four times during the song the A and B parts play the same pitch at the same time. Can you find these places? *(Measures 2, 4, and 6 – E on beat 3. Measure 7 – D on beat 4.)*

Help your child work through each section of **107. Shifting Sands** slowly and carefully. Consider practicing only 1 or 2 of the sections each day.

30

No new skills or symbols are introduced on this page, just 4 more fun songs to play!

Bowing in **109. Natural Beauty Waltz** requires careful planning if your child is going to have enough bow to sustain the dotted half notes.

Measures 1, 3, 9, 11:
- First note: Use a quick, fast down bow starting at the frog.
- Second note: Short up bow in the middle of the bow.
- Third note: Another quick, fast down bow that ends near the tip of the bow.

Measures 2, 4, 10, 12:
- If the bow starts at the tip there will be plenty of bow to sustain each dotted half note for 3 beats.

Before playing **109** with the CD, have your child listen carefully to the bowing style played by the string orchestra. Is the style legato or martelé? *(Legato)* Restart the track and encourage her to match the gentle, relaxed feeling of the music.

Study **110. St. Paul's Steeple**. What is the name of the key? *(D major)* Notice that the first 8 notes of the song are also known as the D major scale. Is the D major scale used in other phrases, too? Help your child use her knowledge of patterns and phrases to memorize this song.

Encourage your child to practice this song with deliberate, martelé strokes. She should work to match the style and mood of the accompaniment. Together can you name some of the other instruments playing? Another day, think of an event that might take place at St. Paul's Cathedral in London at which this song, or something in a similar style, could be performed.

There is also a melodic pattern in **111. The Rock Climber**, starting in the first 2 measures of the song. What happens in measures 3–4? *(The notes in the pattern all move up a step.)* Measures 5–6? *(The notes in the pattern move up another step.)* Have your child play this song with B-naturals the first time, then change to B-flats on the repeat.

Look for melodic patterns in **112. Solo Minuet** as your child practices this piece. She might think of the song in 3 phrases to make it easier to memorize: measures 1–4 (repeated), measures 6–9, and measures 10–14.

Together listen to CD and say the counting as your child "fingers" along. Restart the track and have her play along.

Instrument Care

- String instruments need a certain amount of humidity in the air. Without humidity, the wood dries and shrinks. When it cannot shrink any more, the wood cracks. If you live in a dry climate, ask your teacher about using a humidifier.

100X

Be Creative!

After she has followed the directions in the book for **113.WriteRight Rhythms**, your child can use that rhythm line to write an original composition. Have her take out a piece of manuscript paper.

- On the top staff of the paper, write the clef, D major key signature, and the D major scale in quarter notes (see song **83** on page 24 if needed). Help your child check that she has copied the pitches correctly, and that the stems of the notes are on the correct side of the note head and going the correct direction (up or down). This will be your child's reference line to know which notes can be used for her composition.
- On the next staff line, your child should write the clef, D Major key signature, and $\frac{2}{4}$ time signature.
- Then, she can transfer the rhythm of **113** onto the staff using her choice of notes from the D major scale (written at the top of the staff paper). The first and last notes of the new song must be D. Check that the stems are going the correct direction.
- Have your child play her new composition. If she isn't satisfied with the sound of it, encourage her to change some of the notes and play it again.

114. Boogie Bass suggests the boogie-woogie blues style of the 1930s and 1940s in its repeated, almost hypnotic bass line and 12-bar Blues progression. Together study the notes in this song, and notice that it is only made up of three different arpeggios:

- Measures 1, 2, 3, 4, 7, 8, 11, and 12: G-B-D-E
- Measures 5, 6, and 10: C-E-G(-A)
- Measures 9: D-F♯-A

When your child is able to play **Boogie Bass** confidently, she's ready to play along with the CD. This is a song everyone will enjoy! Encourage her to memorize it as part of her solo repertoire.

Together listen to **115.Weekend Stroll** on the CD. Based on the sound of the music, talk about where the people might be strolling, and what they might see, hear, and smell along the way. Play along, keeping your image in mind.

Find Mexico on the world map in the student book.

Did You Know? Mexico is the world's largest Spanish-speaking country. Its capital, Mexico City, is home to more than 18,000,000 people. Mexico has large mineral deposits of copper, sulfur, lead, and zinc. It is also the world's leading producer of silver.

Remind your young artist to check the key signature before playing **116. Caballito Blanco**, and mark the half steps. How many half steps are there in each part? *(There are 7 half steps in part A, and 6 half steps in part B.)*

Have your child begin songs **117. Brave Knight** and **121. On the Wings of Butterflies** by checking the key signature and time signature. Next have her look for patterns in the notes and rhythms. Ask if any of the patterns repeat. She might clap and count some of the measures, or practice fingering some of the measures with the left hand, before playing each song.

- To complete **118. Composes a Song – Preparation**, your child should have already written (A) the clef sign, (B) three time signatures, (C) two key signatures, (D) different rhythms and rests, and (E) a double bar line.

Here are some additional steps your child might take to complete **119. Compose A Song** (if the orchestra teacher hasn't distributed WriteRight Worksheet III-6).

- Draw the clef (A), copy the key signatures (C), and draw the pitches of each scale. Choose one of these scales for your composition.

    G major   D major

- Copy the time signature (B) you've chosen for your composition at the beginning of the line below. Draw a double bar line at the end. Use the rhythms and rests you know (D) to make up a rhythm line. Check each measure for the correct number of beats. Clap and count it!

- Copy your clef (A), chosen key signature (C), and chosen time signature (B) at the beginning of the staff. Then, transfer your rhythm line onto the staff using notes from the scale you chose. The last pitch of the melody should be the same as the name of the key signature.

- Play your composition. If you are not satisfied, change some of the notes or rhythms and play it again. Once you're satisfied with your song, copy it onto **119. Compose A Song**. Neatness counts! Check for correct stem directions. Don't forget to give your song a title.

33

What's New? Without looking at her book, have your child say and spell each tempo word *(Allegro, Moderato, Andante)*. Then before playing **121. On the Wings of Butterflies,** have her show you how to follow the music with 1st & 2nd endings, and the D.C. al Fine.

Instrument Care

- Never leave a string instrument in the car for an extended period of time when it is very hot or very cold. And, do not store the instrument near a heat vent. Either extreme could cause damage that may be costly to repair.

Recital Time!

Your young artist has reached the end of Unit III, and it's again time to honor her achievement! Perhaps she has already selected several pieces to perform for family or friends.

In preparation for the recital, arrange the room so the soloist and piano accompanist are able to make eye contact, or the accompaniment CD can be heard by everyone. Wipe the rosin dust from the instrument, and check the fingernails.

Prompt your child to introduce the name of each song, along with the name of the composer or its country of origin. At the conclusion of each song, encourage her to look at the audience, smile, and nod to accept their applause.

Record this performance on video tape. Afterwards, watch the tape together and talk about:

- Were songs played accurately?
- Did she stay with the accompaniment?
- Could the audience hear the introduction for each song?

- How was her posture?
- Was the position of the left arm and left hand correct ?
- Was the position of the bow arm and bow hand correct?
- Did the bow stay parallel to the bridge?
- Did she look poised and confident, like she was having fun?

- How did she feel about the performance?
- How did this performance compare to the last one?
- Has memorizing become easier?

UNIT IV – The C- and E-Strings

At the top of page 34, violas and cellos are introduced to notes on their C-string, and violins and basses are introduced to notes on their E-string.

Ask your child to name and play the new notes on this fourth string. Check the placement of his fingers against the photo in the student book.

Have your child play **122. Down 'n' Back Variations** three times today, each time using a different **Slow Bow** rhythm. Another day, have him play **122** as a Meter Melt. You might do the opposite with **124. Up 'n' Back Variations**—today the Meter Melt routine, and tomorrow the three **Slow Bow** rhythms.

Both exercises should be played slowly, with careful attention given to finger placement and intonation.

123. Down 'n' Back Rhythm Mixer is made up of two different phrases, labeled A and B.

- Together talk about ways these phrases are different. *(First, the melodic contour is unique in each phrase. If you trace your finger over the note heads each resulting line has a very different shape. Secondly, the rhythm of each phrase is different.)*
- Do you also see similarities in the phrases? *(Yes, both phrases are 4 measures long, both use notes C-D-E-F, and both seem to have F as the home tone.)*
- If played with repeats (as written), the phrases would be in AABB form, or order. Have your child play song **123** in AABB form. Another day, play it in ABA or AAB form.

125. Up 'n' Back Rhythm Mixer is also written in AABB form. Play this song in ABA and AAB form, too.

Students must be able to play both **123** and **125** confidently at a moderate tempo before playing with the CD. Another day, listen to **123** and write the repeated rhythm pattern of the hand claps.

There are some interesting electronic sounds in the accompaniment for **125**. Have your child select two of the sounds and draw symbols to represent them.

As you listen to **126. The Mountain Climber** with your child, notice the difference between the martelé (1st time) and legato (2nd time) bow strokes. Another day, listen to the CD and, based on the sound of the music, decide if the mountain climber is successful in reaching his goal.

Practice Tip

- A metronome, a small clock-like device that ticks a steady beat at any speed, is an excellent practice partner. It can be used to help a student play at a steady tempo or simply establish the speed indicated in the music.

127. Scales and Arpeggios is made up of two scales and their arpeggios. Together look at part A. Can your child name the two scales? *(C major in measures 1–2, and G major in measures 3–4.)* Then, look at the arpeggios in part B. What two chords are outlined? *(G-chord, G-B-D in measures 1–2, and C-chord, C-E-G in measures 3–4.)* Have him practice each part slowly before playing the entire song.

Songs **128. Poniedziaƚek Rano** and **129. Peter, Peter** are based on the notes of the C major scale.

> **Did You Know?** The note C is the home tone — resting tone, tonic, "do" — of the C major scale and key signature. The final note of a melody in C major will most likely be the tonic C. The C major scale and key signature have no sharps (or flats).

Song **128** is made up of three phrases. Can your child identify each phrase? *(Measures 1–4, 5–8, and 9–12.)* Which phrases are similar? *(The second and third phrases are similar.)* He can use this understanding of the phrases to more easily learn and memorize **Poniedziaƚek Rano**.

Find Poland on the world map in the student book.

> **Did You Know?** Poland's major crops include potatoes, sugar beets, cabbage, fruit, and grains such as wheat and barley. The country is also rich in minerals. The underground salt deposits near Kraków have been mined for more than 1000 years.

As your child plays **128** with the CD or piano accompaniment, evaluate his posture, and the position of the left hand and right hand. Is the bow parallel to the bridge?

After your child is able to play **129. Peter, Peter** as written, he might play "The Disappearing C" game again. Have him substitute rests for all the Cs (both octaves) in the song. Another day, he can play all of the Cs and rest on the other pitches.

Be Creative!
> Take out a piece of manuscript paper. Have your child rewrite **129** as a duet, with one part playing all of the Cs and the other part playing all of the other notes. *(Hint: When one part has a note, the other part must have a rest. Look at **61** as an example of using 2 staff lines to write a duet.)* Play the duet with a friend.

> **Did You Know?** Stephen Foster was born in Pennsylvania. While he was working for his brother as a bookkeeper, he became interested in songwriting. Two of his best remembered songs are "Oh! Susanna" and "Old Folks at Home."

When he is able to play **130. Some Folks Do**, your child will enjoy playing along with this lively accompaniment! Encourage him to memorize this short song.

What's New? Slurs. Until now, students have been using one bow stroke (either up bow or down bow) to play each note. On page 36, students are introduced to 2-note slurs. When there is a curved line connecting two note heads, students will play those two pitches with one bow stroke. Slurring across open strings is easiest, and is executed by raising and lowering the bow arm. Have your child show you how to slur.

Listen to the count-off for **132. Smiles and Rainbows** and clap along to help internalize the pulse. Restart the track and have your child play along. Listen for smooth string crossings.

133. Finger StringSlurs can be played two ways; first as written, and then substituting the small note in parentheses for the original pitch on beat 1. **134. Slurring High, Slurring Low** can be played in different ways, too. Have your child start by playing the song as written, first at a slow tempo, then a little faster. Another day, play the song substituting F-natural and C-natural for the sharp notes.

Did You Know? Jacques Offenbach, a Frenchman, was a fine cellist. He began a career as a soloist and chamber musician while he was still in his teens. In 1850, however, he took a position as conductor at the Théâtre-Français. Five years later he opened his own theater, and began composing operettas. His first great success, "Orpheus in the Underworld," came in 1858.

The entire family may enjoy listening to "Orpheus in the Underworld," as well as many of Offenbach's other works. Borrow recordings from the library or purchase your own.

Your child will enjoy playing 135. Can-Can with the CD. The tempo is slow enough that he should be able to play the slurs accurately, and still convey much of the musical excitement Offenbach intended.

Find the Czech Republic on the world map.

Did You Know? The official one-word name of the Czech Republic is Czechia. Between 1918 and 1993, Czechia was part of Czechoslovakia. In January 1993, two countries were formed—Czech Republic and Slovakia. Bohemia is the western region of Czechia.

Together identify the 4-measure phrases in **136. The Jolly Bohemian**. How are the first and second phrases related? *(The second phrase is either exactly the same as the first, or the same as the first, just moved to another octave.)* How would you represent the form of this song using the letters A and B? *(AABA)* An understanding of the form makes it easier to memorize the song.

Have your child listen to the CD and clap the rhythm of **136**, then restart the track and play along. Another day, he might think of a percussion instrument that could be added to the music.

More slurs, this time in groups of 3! On song **137. Three-String Slurring Roundabout** and song **138. Gentle Waves**, students should concentrate on smooth string crossings.

Have your child listen for the smooth and gentle rolling feeling of **138** on the CD, and match that feeling as he plays along. Watch out for the F-naturals and C-naturals!

Did You Know? Edvard Grieg was born in Bergen, Norway. At the age of 15 he moved to Germany to study piano and music theory. Eventually he returned to his homeland and founded the Norwegian Academy of Music. Grieg continued to perform as a piano soloist, and his compositions started to gain more attention. He was able to create new melodies that reminded people of the charming melodies and dance-like rhythms of the Norwegian folk songs they loved. "Morning Mood" comes from one of Grieg's most popular pieces for orchestra, "Peer Gynt Suite No. 1."

Borrow a recording of "Peer Gynt Suite No. 1" from the library, or purchase a CD for your own collection. As with other classical themes in *Artistry in Strings*, you may be familiar with the music, but do you know the story of Ibsen's character, Peer Gynt? Be sure to read the program notes included with the recording.

Have your child play **139** with the CD or piano accompaniment. Another day, listen to **139** 2–3 times. Imagine you are artists wishing to represent this melody in a picture. What medium would be most appropriate to convey the mood of this song — crayons, chalk, markers, acrylic paints, watercolors, charcoal — and why? Create a picture in your chosen medium to convey "Morning Mood."

140. Keep the Music Ringing is a Hungarian folk song. Find Hungary on the world map in the student book.

Did You Know? Hungary shares its border with 7 countries: Austria, Croatia, Romania, Serbia, Slovakia, Slovenia, and Ukraine. Budapest, the capital city of Hungary, is the country's cultural, political, and commercial center, and home to about 20% of the population.

Together study the 4-measures phrases in **140**. What do you notice? *(The first and second phrases are identical.)* With a friend, play this song as a round.

141. Little Annie is one of seven English folk songs in *Artistry in Strings*. Can your child find the other six? Which **Sports Report** rhythms appear in this song?

Instrument Care

- If you find a crack in the instrument, or an open seam where 2 pieces of the instrument should be joined together, take it to a qualified instrument repair technician. DO NOT attempt to glue it yourself.

38

On page 38, violins and violas begin to use their 4th finger on the D-string. Cellos move into III position. Low Position basses move to Middle Position, and vice versa. All are new and challenging skills that require time to master. Your child will need to go slowly at first. Get out your pom-poms and cheer him on!

Swingercise #11: PinkyPluck was introduced on page 17. Have your child review the photo and instructions, then start **142. PinkyPluck Meter Melt Roundabout** with four left hand plucked quarter notes in each measure. Repeat the song with three quarter notes per measure, then two, then one.

Practice Tip

- If fingers, hands, and arms tire, take a few seconds to shake or wiggle them to relax the muscles.

After your child has practiced each song slowly and carefully, he will enjoy playing along with the CD.

Listen to **143. The Magic Stair**, and have him "finger" along — set his fingers on the string as if to play the notes, but without making a sound. Continue to "finger" along with the CD. When your child can do this easily, and keep up with the melody, add the bow to play the rhythm. Have you noticed the "magical" sound that occurs every time the violins and violas have a G-sharp?

In **145. Fork in the Road**, the pitch of the fingered notes should match the open A-string (measures 2 and 6). If you listen to those measures on the CD, can you hear a difference in the pitches? Have your child "finger" along with the CD, then play aloud.

What does "Allegro" mean? *(See page 33 in the student book.)* Your child will need to know the answer so he is ready to play **146. This Old Man** with the CD. This is an especially fun piece for him to memorize and be able to play for others because they will recognize the song.

Practice Tip

- Sometimes it's fun to begin a practice session by playing a few favorite songs, and some songs that have been memorized.

Instrument Care

- Does the bow need rosin? If you are applying an adequate amount of rosin, rosin dust should be falling onto the top of the instrument. But, remember to wipe off the dust after you play!

Watch for the Fermata ⌢ and *Ritardando* in many songs on this page. They usually appear at or near the end of a song.

Here are several questions to ask your child before he plays song **147. Question Mark Song**:
- What speed should the song go? *(Moderato, moderate speed.)*
- Where is the half step in the first measure? *(Between E and F-natural.)* Can he find 4 more half steps?
- Where do you go after playing the 1ˢᵗ ending? *(Back to the beginning.)*
- What do you do on the last note of the song? *(Hold the note longer than written.)*

Each day your child practices **147**, have him use a different bow stroke — one day legato, martelé the next, then slurring all 3 beats in each measure. Talk about which bowing style you and he like best, and why.

Compare **148. The Contented Cobra** to a song your child learned earlier, **43. Snake Charmer**. Might both have come from a single melody? Even though **148** is written in eighth notes, encourage your child to play it slowly and smoothly, as a contented cobra might move.

Find Jordan on the world map.

> **Did You Know?** Jordan is one of several Arab nations located in the region of the world known as the Middle East. On its western border lies the Dead Sea — 1,300 feet below sea level, and 4 times more salty that ocean water.

As your child learns **149. Happy Children**, have him take time to study the form. How many phrases are there? *(3. The end of each phrase is marked with a bow lift.)* What do you notice about the 1ˢᵗ and 2ⁿᵈ phrases? *(They are identical.)*

Before listening to **149** on the CD, anticipate the tempo of the music. What do you think it might be — Allegro, Moderato, or Andante — and why? Once you've answered this question, listen to the CD. Was your guess correct? Listen again to catch the mood, and play along.

> **Did You Know?** Origami, folding paper into the shapes of animals or other objects, is a distinctive folk art of Japan.

Look for a book at the library or local retail store and make an origami bird in a cage, your own "Kagome."

What bowing style would be most appropriate for **150. Kagome**, legato or martelé? *(Legato)* If your child is unsure, listen to the accompaniment CD and have him match what is heard. He should memorize this song, too.

> **Did You Know?** Thomas Bayly, composer of **151. Long, Long Ago**, was born in Bath, and lived his whole life in England. He made his living as a songwriter, novelist, and dramatist. Very few of his songs are known today.

***Swingercises* #16** and **#17** teach important skills of bow division and bow speed. If your child's teacher hasn't already done so, mark the middle, ¼ and ¾ spots of the bow with chalk or a thin strip of tape. (Remove the tape at the end of the practice session so there is no risk of leaving sticky residue behind.) You can provide the extra set of eyes to help your child play within the specified area of the bow.

#16: Bow Division. Have your child play each exercise on an open string.

    A. Play this exercise using the Whole Bow. On each quarter note, the bow should travel past the ¼ and ¾ marks. Repeat the line using the Middle Bow — staying between the ¼ and ¾ marks. Play it a third time using the Upper Half of the bow — staying between the middle mark and tip of the bow.

    B. In this exercise, the Whole Bow is used for the half notes, and the Upper Half or Lower Half of the bow for the quarter notes. When using the Lower Half of the bow, students play between the middle mark and the frog of the bow.

    C/D. On these lines, the bow needs to travel beyond the ¼ and ¾ marks when Whole Bow is indicated.

#17: Bow Speed. Have your child play each exercise on various open strings, too, always using the Whole Bow. Depending on the value of the note (half note equals 2 beats; quarter note equals 1 beat), the bow will need to go faster or slower to be used up by the end of the note.

Each day this week, have your child practice **152. C Major Scale** using one of the rhythm and bowing patterns from ***Swingercises* #16** and **#17** on each note of the scale. Watch that he is using the part of the bow indicated.

Study **153. Go Tell Aunt Rhodie.** If the melody is made up of 8-measure phrases, what is the form of this song? *(ABA. Even though the rhythms are similar, the melody of the second section seems to move opposite the melody of the first phrase, so we will label the second line B. The* D.C. al Fine *means to go back to the beginning and finish at the end of the measure marked "Fine".)*

Listen to the CD together and follow along on **153** for confirmation of the ABA form. The song begins in rock style (A). At measure 9, it changes to jazz swing style (B), then goes back to rock style with the D.C. al Fine (A). Another day, have your child practice "bow" only with the CD to check he is using WB or UH as indicated. Then, have him "finger" with the CD. Finally, put all the components together, and play along! It's been a long time since Aunt Rhodie had this much fun!

154. Lightly Row provides another opportunity to practice the new fingering introduced on page 38. Ask your child to demonstrate the specified fingering in measures 4 and 7 before playing the entire song. Watch the bow division!

Instrument Care

- If a string is broken and needs to be replaced, ask your teacher for assistance.

Students are introduced to whole notes in **Bow Stroke Rhythms IX – Slowest Bow**. Have your child warm-up by playing whole notes on the open strings. As it moves is the bow staying parallel to the bridge?

Together study the notes in **156. The Towers of Prague**. Which major scale is hidden in the melody? *(C major)* Have your child practice the C major scale so he can play it from memory. Do you or he remember where Bohemia is located? *(Czechia)*

What major scale is hidden in **157. Walrus Waltz**? *(G major)* Have your child practice the G major scale so he can play it from memory. Check the note names your child has written: *G-A-B C-B A-B-C D G-F♯-E D-E C-B-A B G*

When your child is able to play **Walrus Waltz** smoothly and confidently, using a legato bow stroke and slurring one bow per measure, he is ready to be accompanied by the CD. Another day, listen to the recording together and, based on the sound of the music, rename the song after a different animal.

Practice Tip

- As you listen to your child practice, do you hear a hesitation or mistake? Encourage him to practice the difficult measure or measures over and over until he can play them correctly. Then, play the song all the way through.

Ask your child to name the key signature for **158. Country Gardens**. *(C major)* Is that also the name of the major scale hidden in the melody? *(Yes)*

Before playing with the CD, have your child listen to it and decide the tempo at which the song was recorded — Andante, Moderato, or Allegro. *(Allegro)* If he has trouble keeping up with the accompaniment at that speed, have him practice a bit more alone, and then try it again.

Did You Know? Franz Joseph Haydn held a position in the Court of the Esterházy family for most of his adult life. He was employed as a servant to provide four formal concerts each week. Most often, the pieces performed at these concerts were Haydn's own compositions. In his lifetime he composed many works for the keyboard, several operas, 104 symphonies, and 43 string quartets.

Borrow a recording of Haydn's entire Symphony No. 104 from the library, or purchase a CD for your own collection. Can you determine the movement from which **159** was taken?

159. Theme – Symphony No. 104 is a good song to memorize and play for others.

Instrument Care

- If a peg is slipping so the string will not stay in tune, inform your child's teacher.

Practice Tip

- Practice a song slowly before playing it at a faster tempo.

Did You Know? Ludwig van Beethoven was born in Germany, and moved to Vienna, Austria at the age of 22. His early career there was quite successful. Beethoven made his living as one of the first "freelance" musicians, by giving concerts, teaching piano lessons, and publishing music. He composed only one violin concerto. The first performance of this concerto was given in 1806, four years after Beethoven's hearing began to fail.

Borrow a recording of Beethoven's Violin Concerto from the library, or purchase a CD for your own collection. When you listen to the concerto, you will notice that the solo violin and the orchestra take turns playing the melody.

Did someone sing lullabies to your child when he was a baby? Can you remember one of the lullabies and sing it now? If so, compare the melody, rhythm, and style of your song to the CD recording of **161. Iroquois Lullaby.** How are they similar? How are they different? Another day, have your child play along with the accompaniment.

162. Shalom, Chaverim is an Israeli folk song. Find Israel on the world map.

Did You Know? People of Israel enjoy all kinds of outdoor activities, including whitewater rafting on the Jordan River, and rappelling down cliffs in the Negev Desert. The Negev Desert, in southern Israel, is also where the Ramon Crater is located. This crater was caused by erosion, and covers an area of more than 110 square miles.

163. A La Puerta del Cielo is a Spanish folk song. Find Spain on the world map.

Did You Know? The only European country more mountainous than Spain is Switzerland. The rugged terrain has made travel and communications difficult within the country. That is the major reason why Spain is still a country of many distinct regions.

Before playing **163** with the CD, have your child listen and follow along in the music. What happens on the fermata in measure 14? **A La Puerta del Cielo** is a good song to have memorized.

Be Creative!

After he has followed the directions in the book for **164. WriteRight Rhythms**, have your child improvise a simple song using the rhythm line, the note C, and one other note in the C major scale. Play **164** again using C and two other notes of the C scale. Another day, suggest he use C and three or four other notes of the C scale. Play it slow, play it fast! These improvised songs will have a sense of finality if the last note is C.

 Have your child listen to the accompaniment before playing along, and notice the lively, energetic feeling of the music. **165. Pop! Goes the Weasel** will be even more fun to listen to if special attention is given to the rests. Have him memorize this song.

 Encourage your child to count confidently as he plays **166. Rest Stop** with the CD. This should be included in his repertoire of memorized songs, too.

Here are some additional steps your child might take to complete **167. Compose A Song** (if the orchestra teacher hasn't distributed WriteRight Worksheet IV-7).

- Draw your clef, the key signature, and major scale you would like to use for your song.

- Choose a time signature for your composition, and write it at the beginning of the line. Draw a double bar line at the end. Use ♩, 𝄽, ♫, ♩, ♩., and o to create your own rhythm line. Make sure the last measure has a feeling of "the end." Check each measure for the correct number of beats. Clap and count it!

- On another piece of paper, transfer your rhythm line onto the staff using notes from the major scale you've chosen. (Don't forget to write your clef sign and key signature on both lines, and the time signature at the beginning of the first staff.)
- Check your work! Is the last pitch of the melody the same as the name of the key signature? Are all the stems going in the correct direction?
- Play your composition. If you are not satisfied with the sound of it, change some of the notes and play it again. When you are satisfied with your song, copy it into your book on **167. Compose A Song**. Neatness still counts! Don't forget to give it a title, and indicate a tempo that best matches your composition.

Did You Know? Johannes Brahms was born in Hamburg, Germany. He learned about music and music theory from his father who played double bass in the Hamburg orchestra. Johannes also took piano lessons, and was performing public concerts by the age of 10. In 1853 he played a concert tour with a famous Hungarian violinist, and shortly thereafter, Brahms began to work on a set of 21 *Hungarian Dances* for piano, 4-hands. Throughout his career, he composed various types of music—4 symphonies and other works for orchestra, many chamber works and pieces for solo piano, and even more choral works. It wasn't until after his death, however, that people recognized Brahms's high level of achievement.

Look for recordings of Brahms's music at the library, a local retail store, or online.

Recital Time!

Your young artist has reached the end of Unit IV, and has many more songs to play for others! If your child feels comfortable in doing so, look for new opportunities for him to perform—a home day care in the neighborhood, a scout meeting, a special sharing day in your place of worship, a talent day at school.

Depending on the situation, your child's program might include 1–4 songs. Guide his selection of songs for variety— classical theme, folk song, original composition, slow song, fast song, fun song!

Help your child prepare an introduction for each song. He should announce the name of the song, and the name of the composer or its country of origin. He might also say a sentence or two about the song such as why he chose to play it, or what was learned from practicing it.

Your child should practice the songs with the CD or piano accompaniment to be comfortable and confident in the tempos. He should also continue to practice the songs without the accompaniment to review technique. He might check posture and hand positions by practicing a short time in front of a mirror.

The actual performance should be fun if your child is well prepared. Encourage your child to dress-up a bit — this is a special day! You can help by remembering to bring the CD player, accompaniment CDs and an extension cord.

Record this performance on videotape. Afterwards, watch the tape together and talk about how his playing has improved since the last recital.

UNIT V – Onward and Upward!

Have your child demonstrate the bouncing spiccato stroke introduced on this page. Does the bow remain perpendicular to the strings (parallel to the bridge)? For the best sound, it should.

Your child should start **170. Bounceabout Meter Melt** with four spiccato quarter notes in each measure. Repeat the song with three spiccato quarter notes per measure, then two, then one. Spiccato bow stroke is easier to execute when the tempo is fairly fast.

Have your child practice **171. Three-String Spiccato** using a metronome to maintain a steady pulse.

Together listen to **171** on the CD. Count "1-&-2-&" as your child pantomimes spiccato with an imaginary bow, then restart the track and have her play along. Encourage her to match the mood of the accompaniment and have fun playing this song!

Compare **172. French Fried Spiccato** to **84. Chanson Populaire Française**. Your child's fingers already know what to do so she can concentrate on the spiccato bowing (**172** presents different fingerings for bass players). Watch that the bow stays parallel to the bridge. Can your child name the key signature of this song? *(D major)*

As he plays **172** with the accompaniment, encourage your child to synchronize the eighth notes with the steady rhythm of the temple blocks and accordion. Another day, listen to the accompaniment 2–3 times. What other instruments do you hear? What feeling do you get from the music? Based on these impressions (and the title), talk about the type of food your family might be served at a restaurant if you heard **French Fried Spiccato** as background music.

Others would enjoy hearing **172. French Fried Spiccato**. Encourage your child to memorize this song as part of her solo repertoire.

Be Creative!

Take out a piece of manuscript paper. Have your child copy **172**, but change the rhythm in each measure to ♩♫ ♩ or ♫ ♩ ♩. Can she play the new song with the CD?

Practice Tip

- Be sure there is time in each practice session to play some favorite songs and the ones that have been memorized. With or without the accompaniment, memorized or read from the book, it's fun to go back and review earlier songs.

Practice Tip

- The best place to practice is a quiet place—away from the television, telephone, computer, and other disruptions. A music stand raised to the proper height, and an appropriate size chair or stool, will also help make practice time productive.

What's New? Double stops. Notice the double stops in **173–178** are played on adjacent open strings.

Tell me more about intervals.
An interval is the distance between two notes or pitches. To name an interval, begin with the lowest note (counted as "1") and count each line and space up to (and including) the highest note.

Each of the following intervals is a 2nd. Seconds are either called a half step or a whole step.

Have your child draw her instrument's clef next to the 2nds, then name the notes. Which pair of notes is a half step and which is a whole step?

(Violins: Half step = middle pair of notes; Violas: Half step = 3rd pair of notes; Cellos/Basses: Half step = 1st pair of notes.)

Here's another Meter Melt. Have your child play **174. Double Stop Meter Melt Roundabout** four times through—first with four quarter notes per measure, then three, then two, then one.

As your child plays **175. Tunin' Country** with the CD, encourage her to match the confident and energetic feeling of the accompaniment. Then, talk about the tempo marking given to this melody. Does she like to play it at the tempo of the CD, or does she like to play it faster?

Together listen to **177. Strawberry Pie, Oh My!** on the CD. Can you hear the difference between the martelé, spiccato, and legato bow strokes? At what tempo do you think the recording was made—Allegro, Moderato, or Andante? *(Moderato)*

Strawberry Pie, Oh My! (in ¾ meter) and "Mary Had a Little Lamb" (in ⁴⁄₄ meter) begin with the same four pitches. Challenge your child to play "Mary Had a Little Lamb" by ear. He might also try playing "The First Noel" and "Jolly Old St. Nicholas" by ear, starting on the same pitches. Can you think of other songs that start with the same notes?

Instrument Care

- Avoid letting someone other than your young musician play her instrument.

47

More double stops!

Practice Tip

- At the end of the practice session, have your child think back about her playing today—the rhythm, bowing, intonation. "What improved today?" and "Which songs or skills need work tomorrow?"

179. Scales with Double Stops is the first double-stop song where one of the two notes is "stopped" by a finger. Encourage your child to work for a clear tone by using equal bow weight on each string. Check the names of the intervals he has written in the book: 5th-4th-3rd-2nd (also a whole step) 5th-6th-7th-8th (also an octave).

Encourage your child to hold the tempo steady as she plays **181. Horn Call** with the CD. The quarter notes must be played deliberately and spaced so they don't rush. Another day, listen again and talk about the differences you hear between the first time through and the repeat.

182. Frank's Friendly Fiddle Factory is a song students will want to memorize and have as part of their solo repertoire. Encourage your child to join the fun as he plays along with this "down home" accompaniment.

Did You Know? Gioacchino Rossini was born in Italy on February 29, leap-year day. His father played trumpet and other brass instruments in the theaters, and his mother was an opera singer. As a child, Gioacchino learned to play the French horn, violin, viola, and harpsichord, and studied singing and music theory. He began composing music in his teenage years. At the age of 23, Rossini composed "The Barber of Seville," still considered by many to be his greatest opera. "William Tell" premiered in 1829, and was very popular, too. He stopped writing operas at the age of 37, and turned his attention to composing piano pieces, vocal solos, and other instrumental works. His home in a suburb of Paris became a gathering place for musicians and artists.

183. William Tell is written in $\frac{4}{4}$ time. Why are there only 3 beats in the last measure? *(The fourth beat was taken from the last measure and used as a pick-up note at the beginning of the song.)*

Have your child listen to **183** on the CD 2–3 times, and write the rhythm pattern played on the suspended cymbal. *(Hint: In measures 1–7 the same pattern is repeated, but the pattern changes in the last measure.)* Of course, she will want to play along with the accompaniment, too.

100X

Ask your child to explain ties. He might clap and play the **What's New?** example for you, too, as part of the explanation. *(You should hear 5 sounds when he does this, the middle sound being 2 beats long.)*

185. Barcarolle was written by Jacques Offenbach. Can you and your child remember the name of another song in the book by Offenbach?

> **Did You Know?** Offenbach's only grand opera, "The Tales of Hoffman," was unfinished when he died in 1880. Another composer added recitatives and re-used the "Barcarolle" Jacques had composed in 1864. "The Tales of Hoffman" was an immediate success!

> **Did You Know?** Gustav Mahler was born in Bohemia. He studied piano, harmony, and composition at the Vienna Conservatory. In 1880, Mahler got his first job as a conductor. As his abilities became more refined, he held important conducting positions in several European cities. In 1907, Mahler moved to New York City, where he conducted the New York Philharmonic and Metropolitan Opera orchestras.

Acquire a recording of Mahler's Symphony No. 1 and listen to the entire work. Others will enjoy hearing your child play this beautiful, haunting theme from the 3rd movement from memory.

Before playing **186. Theme – Symphony No. 1** with the CD, have your child count along to internalize the pulse. Another day, listen to the accompaniment and have her move a hand to show the changing volume — the higher the hand is raised, the louder the volume.

Together listen to **187. Slavonic Dance** and notice the difference in the sound of the first and second phrases. Which pitches cause the differences in sound? *(F-natural and F-sharp)*

Be Creative!

After he has followed the directions in the book for **189. WriteRight Rhythms**, your child can use the rhythm line as the basis for an original composition. Notice how the rhythms in measures 1–4 seem to make one musical idea, and those in measures 5–8 make another idea. Take out a piece of staff paper.

- On the top staff, your child can write the clef, the G key signature, and G scale.
- On the next staff line, she can write the clef, G key signature, and $\frac{3}{4}$ time signature. She is ready to transfer the rhythm of **189** using her choice of notes from the G scale. She might use the first few notes of the scale in the first phrase, and the higher notes of the scale in the second phrase. This will help differentiate between the phrases. The last note of the new song must be G. Check the note stems.
- Have your child play her new composition. If she isn't satisfied with the sound of it, encourage her to change some of the notes and play it again.

Students are introduced to three dynamic levels on this page. Have your child demonstrate how her orchestra teacher instructed the class to play loud, moderately loud, then soft.

Practice Tip

- Before playing a new song for the first time, check the key signature, the time signature, look for measures with unusual rhythms or complicated note patterns, and check for specific bowings. After all of these elements are taken care of, add dynamics as indicated.

Before playing **190. Yankee Doodle** with the CD, have your child listen to the music and notice the changes in dynamics that occur in measures 9 and 13. Another day, listen together and identify the instrument playing the high "twittery" countermelody beginning in measure 9. *(Piccolo)*

Locate Nigeria on the world map.

> **Did You Know?** Nigeria is home to more than 126,000,000 people, representing 250 ethnic groups. Each group has its own traditions of music and dance. Music plays an important role in the way each of the groups remembers their past and celebrates their present.

191. Kum Ba Yah looks fairly simple, but the longer notes (ones sustained for 4, 5, and 6 beats) are challenging to play. Have your child play the rhythm of this song on an open string, and concentrate on bowing so she can play each note to its full value. Do you see both a slur and tie in involving measures 13–14?

While your child is still learning **191**, have her sing the melody (on "lah") with the CD to help internalize the rhythm of the long notes. Next listen for the changes in dynamics, and begin to attend to those as the rhythm and pitches are mastered. She should memorize this song.

Locate Scotland on the world map.

> **Did You Know?** Golf originated in Scotland. The British Open Championship is played every year in the city of St. Andrews. Scotland is home to many lakes (lochs). The largest one is Loch Lomond, near Glasgow.

Have your child listen to **192. Loch Lomond** on the CD, and think of a word or phrase to describe the mood of the song. Encourage her to keep that mood in mind as she plays along. Watch out for the ritard! Another day, note the changes in dynamics in measures 4 and 6.

Have your child study **193. Chorale** before he starts to play. What is the name of the key signature? *(C major)* How many beats are in each measure? *(4)* What is the speed of this song? *(Andante - moderately slow)* Which measures might be the most tricky to play? *(Perhaps measures 4 and 6 with the accidentals in the Ensemble part, and the slurs in measures 6 and 7.)* When do the dynamics change? *(Measures 5 and 7)*

Locate Australia on the world map. Your child will enjoy playing **194. Botany Bay** with friends.

Did You Know? In 1770, Captain James Cook, an Englishman, discovered the eastern part of Australia. He named one coastal area Botany Bay because of the wide variety of plants growing along the shores in "as fine a meadow as ever was seen." Most of the early inhabitants of Botany Bay were convicted criminals, banished to this far-off land from Great Britain.

---

195. The Mountain Goat Song provides a good review of bowing styles. Have your child play the song several times, each time with a different bow stroke. Another day, listen from another room as she plays. Can you tell if she is playing legato, martelé, or slurring the notes in groups of two without looking? There is a D major scale hidden in this song. Can your child find it? *(It starts on beat 2, measure 6.)*

Practice Tip

- A second set of ears often hears different elements of a performance. Encourage your spouse or another significant adult to participate in your child's practice sessions, too.

Listen to **197. When the Saints Go Marching In**. Have your child name the instruments in this Dixieland Band, then join the fun! Did he notice on what beat the song starts? *(The song has three pick-up notes, and starts on beat 2.)*

Instrument Care

- When the practice or rehearsal is finished, loosen the bow, and wipe any rosin from the bow stick and surface of the instrument with a soft cloth. Store the instrument and bow securely.

Ask your child what kind of bow strokes should be used after the first measure in **198. Henry Harmonic**? *(Martelé)* What kind of bow strokes should be used after the second measure in **199. She'll Be Comin" Round the Mountain**? *(Spiccato)*

Recital Time!

Your young artist has almost reached the end of Unit V and *Artistry in Strings* Book 1. She has many songs to play for others — some favorite songs with or without accompaniment, and many others that have been memorized. Encourage your child to perform often, at informal family recitals, adjudicated festivals, and for every audience in between. Review **Recital Time!** on page 44. A final word of caution: Honor the fine line between supporting and pressuring; between enjoying your child's accomplishments and living through them!

51

Here are some steps your child might take to complete **200. Compose A Song** (if the orchestra teacher hasn't distributed WriteRight Worksheet V-5).

- Write your clef, the key signature (G, C, or D), and corresponding major scale you would like to use for your song.

- Choose ¾ or 4/4 time signature for your composition, and write it at the beginning of the line. Use ♩, 𝄽, ♫, ♩, ♩., and o to create your rhythm line made up of two 4-measure phrases. Make sure the last measure has a feeling of "the end." Draw a double bar line at the end. Check each measure for the correct number of beats. Clap and count it!

- Transfer your rhythm line onto the staff using notes from the major scale you've chosen. You might use the first few notes of the scale in the first phrase, and the higher notes of the scale in the second phrase. (Don't forget to write your clef sign and key signature on both lines, and the time signature only on the first staff.)
- Add at least two slurs. Indicate the tempo, dynamics, and any other musical markings you wish. Give your composition a title.
- Check your work. Is the last pitch of the melody the same as the name of the key signature? Are the stems going the correct direction?
- Play your composition. If you are not satisfied with the sound of it, change some of the notes and play it again. When you are satisfied with your song, copy it neatly into your book on **200. Compose A Song**. Neatness still counts!

Practice Tip

- Your child's fingernails must be short if she is going to be able to press the strings firmly into the fingerboard.

 Like songs **59** and **114, 201. Rockin' & Rollin'** is based on a 12-bar Blues progression. As your child is practicing this song, have her name the intervals of the double stops. Then, put on the CD and join the fun! Have her memorize this song to have in her solo repertoire.

Did You Know? Robert Frost, one of the composers of *Artistry in Strings*, used melodies by Jacques Offenbach and Modest Mussorgsky to create **202. The Rhythm of the Dance**. Modest Mussorgsky lived his entire life in Russia. He earned his living by working in various government jobs, and composed on the side. From his work, and that of several other Russian composers, came a new style of music that was based on traditional Russian folk melodies. Two of Mussorgsky's best known works are "A Night on Bald Mountain" and "Pictures at an Exhibition."

Do you and your child recognize Offenbach's theme that begins in measure 18 of **The Rhythm of the Dance**? *("Can-Can" from the opera <u>Orpheus in the Underworld</u>)*

Down
1. Hold note or rest longer than written
2. Notes of a chord played one at a time
3. Cancels a sharp or flat
5. Play with the bow
8. Music with different parts for 2 players
10. Note before the first full measure
13. The softness or loudness of music
14. Moderate speed
17. Pitch distance between two notes
18. Whole Bow
20. The speed of music
21. Crisp bow stroke that starts with the bow deeply planted into the string
22. Raises a natural note ½ step
25. Cool, flute-like tones made by touching the string lightly at certain places

Across
2. Moderately slow
4. Two or more notes connected smoothly in one bow
6. Slur mark joining 2 notes of the same pitch, which then become one long note
7. Players play the same melody but begin at different times
9. Fast and lively
11. Lowers a natural note ½ step
12. Play by plucking the string
14. Middle of the Bow
15. Upper half of the bow
16. Gradually slow the tempo
19. Two notes played together by one player
22. Continue playing in the same way
23. Lower Half of the bow
24. Interval between a note and the next lowest or highest note with the same name
26. Play smoothly connected
27. Soft
28. Moderately loud
29. Bounced bow stroke

How much have YOU learned? Complete this MUSICAL TERMS crossword puzzle on your own using the clues on page 52. Enlist the help of your child only when you are stumped!

Congratulations on your completion of the **Parent's Guide for**

Artistry in Strings
Book 1

May you and your special child share a lifetime of music together!

Wendy Barden

Reference

Tuning the Instrument

Tuning a string instrument before playing is essential. Tuning the string means comparing its sound to a fixed pitch, such as a tuning note track on the *Artistry in Strings* CD accompaniment recording, or notes on the piano or a pitch pipe, and adjusting the string to match that pitch.

Your child's teacher will show students the process he or she prefers, but here are two ways you can tune a VIOLIN, VIOLA, or CELLO at home.

You can change the pitch of each string by turning the peg or the string adjuster (at the tailpiece). When an adjuster is screwed in, it tightens the string and the pitch sounds higher. When a peg is turned away from you, the string winds tighter and the pitch sounds higher.

1. Hold the instrument to face you as shown in the drawings on the next page. Play the A tuning track on the *Artistry in Strings* Accompaniment Recordings, or sound A on a piano or pitch pipe. Listen, then sing the pitch. Pluck the A string. Decide if the string should be adjusted higher or lower to match the sound of the tuning note.

2. To raise the pitch with the string adjuster, turn it clockwise about ¼ turn (to screw it in and tighten the string), and compare it to the sound of the CD. Alternate between the tuning pitch and the string's pitch until the sounds seem to match. If the sound is too high, turn the adjuster counterclockwise (to loosen the string), and continue to check it. Periodically, look to see that the string adjusters have not been turned clockwise so much that they are digging into the top of the instrument. Your child's teacher can remedy this situation.

3. CAUTION! It is easy to over tune and break a string when tuning with the peg. Having said that, to change the pitch with the peg, take hold of the A peg with your right hand. Turn it towards you to slightly loosen the string, then slowly turn the peg away from you to raise the pitch. As you turn the peg, you should be testing the pitch by plucking with your thumb. When you stop turning the peg, if the sound is still too high or too low, start again.

4. Tune the other three strings of the instrument before your child begins to play.

Violin

Tailpiece

Viola

Cello

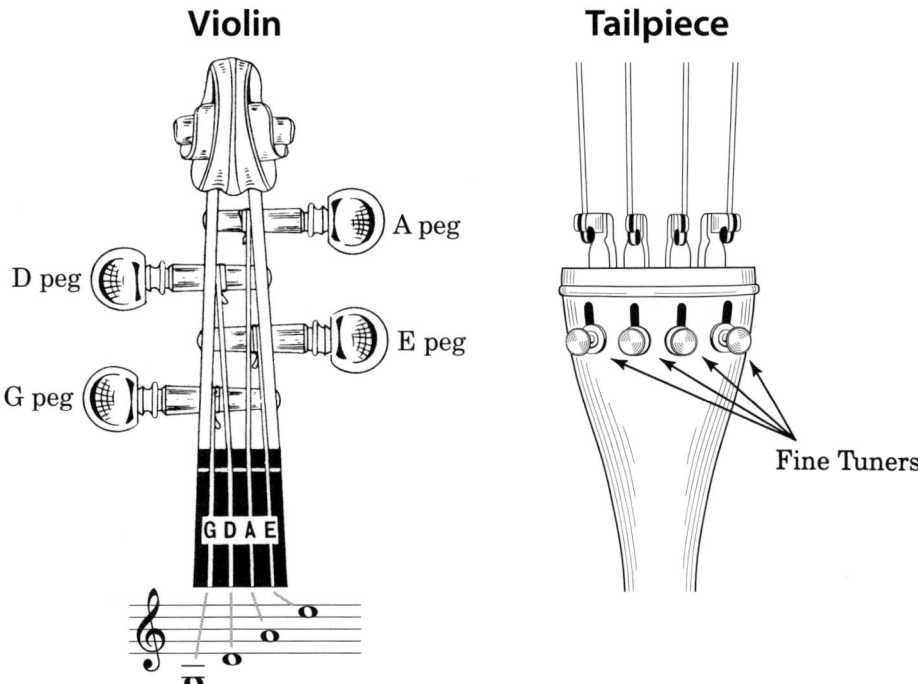

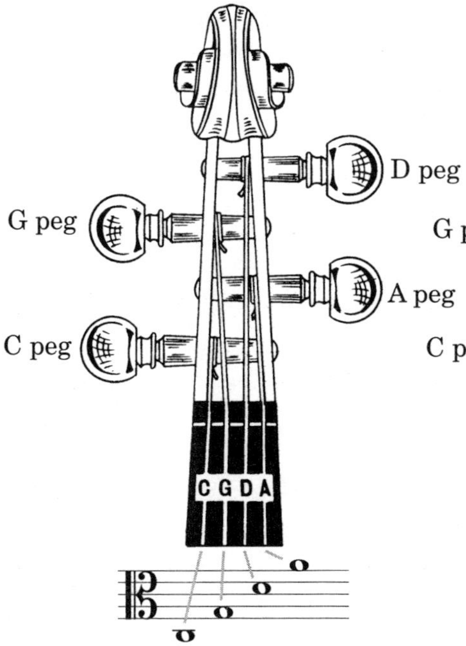

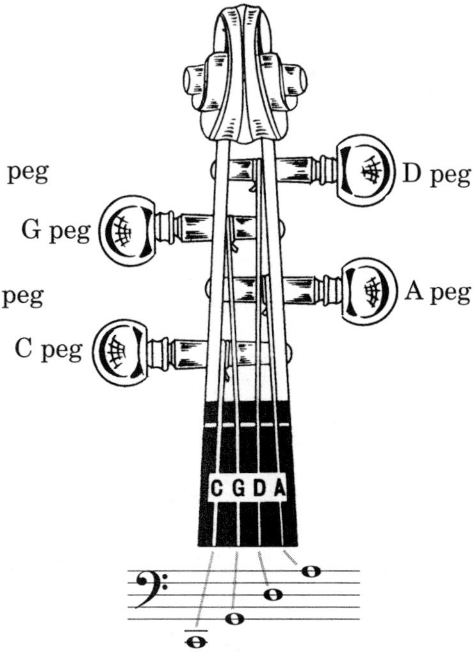

You can also tune a BASS at home.

1. Hold the instrument as if you are going to play a song. Play the A tuning track on the *Artistry in Strings* CD, or sound A on a piano or pitch pipe. Listen, then sing the pitch. Pluck the A string. Decide if the string should be adjusted higher or lower to match the sound of the tuning note.

2. Take hold of the A peg with your left hand. When held in this position, if a peg is turned clockwise, the string loosens and the pitch sounds lower. When a peg is turned counterclockwise, the string tightens and the pitch is raised. As you turn the peg, you should be testing the pitch by plucking the string. When you stop turning the peg, if the sound is still too high or too low, start again.

3. All 4 strings should be tuned before your child is ready to play.

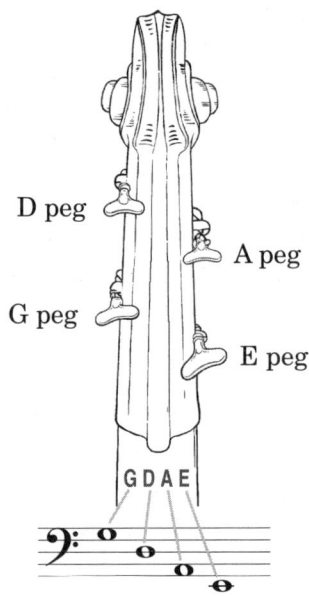

Practice Tips

- Set up a regular time for practicing. Many young musicians choose to practice at the same time every day, like before school or right after dinner. The best place is a quiet place, away from the television, telephone, computer, and other disruptions. When your child practices, remain nearby to monitor and support her work.
- Using a music stand allows a musician to be able to sit or stand tall and hold the instrument correctly.
- If fingers, hands, and arms tire, take a few seconds to shake or wiggle them to relax the muscles.
- Take time in each practice session to play some favorite songs!
- Each day, review the teacher's feedback and instructions given on an assignment sheet, on the pages of the lesson book, and on the Assessment Record.
- Your child's fingernails must be short if she is going to be able to press the strings firmly into the fingerboard and sound with a resonant tone.
- Encourage your child to stop and practice difficult measures over and over until she can play them correctly. Then, play the song all the way through.
- At the end of each practice session, your child should be able to answer two questions, "What improved today?" and "Which songs or skills need work tomorrow?"
- A second set of ears often hears different elements of a performance. Encourage your spouse or another significant adult to participate in your child's practice sessions, too.
- Before playing a new song for the first time, check the key signature, the time signature, look for measures with unusual rhythms or complicated note patterns, check the speed, and check for specific bowings.
- Record daily practice time on a chart or calendar. Set weekly or monthly practice goals and reward diligent effort.
- Students often stand when playing their violins or violas at home. Cellists need a proper size chair. Bass students might stand or sit on a stool, based on their teachers' recommendation.
- Initially, daily practice session should be 10–15 minutes in length. As hand and arm strength improves, and skills become more complex, increase the length of practice session to 20–30 minutes.
- A metronome, a small clock-like device that ticks a steady beat at any speed, is an excellent practice partner. It can be used to help a student play at a steady tempo or simply establish the speed indicated in the music.
- Practice a song slowly before taking it at a fast tempo.
- Make practicing more fun by playing along with the *Artistry in Strings* CD Accompaniment Recordings. Warning! A student must be able to play a song confidently, and at the appropriate tempo before adding the accompaniment.
- Do you, or another member of your family, play piano? Get the *Artistry in Strings* Piano Accompaniment Book at your local music store, and enjoy making music together. Every song in the student book has a piano accompaniment.

Instrument Care

- String instruments and bows must be handled with care.

- Avoid letting someone other than your young musician play his instrument.

- Apply rosin lightly over the entire length of the bow as necessary.

- When the practice or rehearsal is finished, loosen the bow, and wipe any rosin from the bow stick and surface of the instrument with a soft cloth. Store the instrument and bow securely.

- Avoid touching the bow hair.

- Store the instrument away from heating and cooling vents, and out of the direct sunlight.

- Avoid leaving a string instrument in the car when it is very hot or very cold for extended periods of time. Either extreme could cause damage.

- String instruments need a certain amount of humidity in the air. Without humidity, the wood dries and shrinks. When it cannot shrink any more, the wood cracks. If you live in a dry climate, ask your teacher about using a humidifier.

- A crack in the instrument, or an open seam where 2 pieces of the instrument have come unglued, often causes a "buzz" when played. Take it to a qualified instrument repair technician. DO NOT attempt to glue it yourself.

- Keep a record of the instrument's serial number (look inside the f-holes). Be sure the instrument is covered by your homeowner's insurance.

- Attach a nametag to the case.

- If a peg is slipping so the string will not stay in tune, inform your child's teacher.

- If the instrument needs a string replaced, ask your child's teacher for assistance.

There's Always More to Learn!

How Should I Choose a Private Lesson Teacher?

When your child is ready for private lessons, choose a music teacher as carefully as you would a daycare provider or financial planner. These professionals provide services to meet an individual's needs, and a good private music teacher will do the same. Ask to interview a prospective teacher and observe a lesson with another student. Answers to the following questions will help you select a person who will nurture your child's musical skill and love of music.

- Is there a comfortable rapport between the student and teacher?
- Are the teacher's comments made in such a way as to be both corrective and supportive?
- Does the teacher show a good understanding of string technique?
- Is the teacher able to model various techniques easily?
- Is there a particular age or skill level of student with whom the teacher feels most comfortable working?
- What does the teacher expect of the student in terms of home practice?
- What performance opportunities does the teacher facilitate, such as recitals and adjudicated events?
- What does the teacher expect of parents?
- What is the teacher's policy for missed lessons?

Look for Opportunities to Listen and Learn!

- Listen to both live and recorded music—all styles! Many public libraries have them for check-out, or you might choose to develop your own family collection of recordings.
- Attend a concert or recital of students close to your child's age.
- Attend a concert by the high school orchestra, community orchestra, or professional orchestra.
- Attend a musical and take the opportunity to look in the pit to see the musicians.
- Books about composers can bring new meaning to playing a string instrument.
- Does your child have a Social Studies, History, or English assignment that could incorporate her love of music?
- When you are traveling, stop and visit a museum. Look for string instruments in the collection, and paintings of musicians or instruments.
- Attend a local festival or fair, and seek out musical performances.
- Attend a movie, and pay attention to the orchestral soundtrack.
- Listen to a classical FM radio station such as National Public Radio.

CALLING ALL PARENTS

25 PROVEN METHODS
For Ruining Your Child's Music Education*

1. Buy him the cheapest instrument possible so that he can "look forward" to "earning" a better one.

2. Always point out *all* of his shortcomings; *never* praise. "There's no sense in spoiling him."

3. Always call him for practice when the ball game's going best; call in a loud, demanding voice so his friends will feel sorry for him.

4. Insist he practice a certain time each day without exception. Lay down the law. "Either you practice when I say, or you quit!"

5. Insist he practice the most uninteresting music the longest. "You can't learn to play an instrument by playing tunes!"

6. Don't invite other children in to play instruments with your child. They make too much "noise," "kill" too much time, have too much "fun,"—and track in too much dirt!

7. Be sure to tell Father at the dinner table how Little Son has practiced. Then he won't dare leave anything on his plate.

8. Never help him with his practicing. "I just never have the time."

9. Add another hour of practice when he has been naughty, or doesn't mind you.

10. Call loudly from the kitchen or basement each time he makes a mistake. Add a punch line such as, "Was that a sick cat I heard?" or "If you can't do better than that, better give up."

11. Stop him if he practices anything for fun other than his lesson. "Music is serious!"

12. Threaten, periodically, to stop his lessons, unless: (a) he practices much more, (b) he plays better than so-and-so, (c) he takes better care of his instrument, (d) he makes better grades, (e) he makes his bed each morning, (f) he treats his parents with more respect.

13. Insist on perfection in everything connected with his music. 100% or it's no good. "He'll appreciate this when he grows up."

14. Don't let him play for his friends or anybody else until he can really play his instrument. After two or three years he'll be able to "surprise" them.

15. Take him unawares the first time you want him to play for someone and ask him in front of everybody to play "something." If he refuses, insist that he play; if he still refuses, announce that he's through with music. By all means, don't help him select and work up a number which he can play for company.

16. Don't take him to a concert until he's old enough, and don't take him unless he can play well enough to "appreciate" it.

17. Insist that he take private lessons from the strictest, driest teacher in town.

18. Be sure to point out his shortcomings often, especially in front of teacher or fellow students. "It will make a better impression then."

19. Rest your nerves after a hard day's work by telling him not to practice where you can hear him. "Take that thing down to the basement. Don't I deserve a little peace and quiet?"

20. Insist that he can't take band or orchestra unless his grades improve in his academic subjects. "Band is just play anyhow."

21. Insist that he take Latin in high school instead of band or orchestra. "After all, Latin is required for college entrance!"

22. Don't pay attention to his music making; you don't care whether he practices or not.

23. Use music as a wedge for getting other things done; e.g., if he doesn't wash the dishes every night, threaten to cut off his lessons.

24. Don't buy him a good instrument until he plays "real well." "No sense wasting money!"

25. With some parents, the real secret is to nag effectively and regularly. Others manage to ruin their child's music making by disregarding it almost completely. "If my child likes it, O.K. If not, O.K." Strangely enough, the over-ambitious parent succeeds with amazing consistency!

*It is not necessary to apply all 25. Usually one or two will do the job.

©1951 by *The Instrumentalist* Magazine.
Used with permission.